To Jeannie and Tina

Churches and How to Survive Them

RICHARD HOLLOWAY has been Bishop of Edinburgh since 1986. He is a frequent broadcaster and for four years presented the popular television series *When I Get To Heaven*. He writes regularly for a number of journals and newspapers, and is a well-known preacher who has conducted university missions in many parts of the world, including Oxford, Glasgow and Harvard. *Churches And How To Survive Them* is his fourteenth and a half book.

BRICE AVERY is a child and family psychiatrist and an adult psychoanalytic psychotherapist. A member of the Group-analytic Society and the Royal College of Psychiatrists, he consults on institutional dynamics to churches, corporations and small businesses. Brice is a committed member of his local church where he regularly preaches and leads seminars. He is married and lives in Scotland.

Churches
And How To Survive Them

Richard Holloway and Brice Avery

Illustrated by Nick Newman

HarperCollins*Publishers*

HarperCollins*Publishers*
77-85 Fulham Palace Road
Hammersmith, London W6 8JB

First published in Great Britain in 1994
by HarperCollins*Publishers*
1 3 5 7 9 10 8 6 4 2

A catalogue record for this book
is available from the British Library

ISBN 0 551 02855-6

Typeset by Harper Phototypesetters Limited
Northampton, England
Printed and bound in Great Britain by
HarperCollinsManufacturing Glasgow

Contents

Introduction

Why We Wrote This Book

Brice A few years ago it struck me that many of the frustrations and difficulties encountered in the Church could be investigated from a psychodynamic point of view. After further thought I realized that the best way to thrash this stuff out was in a dialogue between myself and a practical theologian. At that time I had no idea whom to invite to help. Then, one day, I asked Richard if he could suggest anyone suitable; he could and he did. So what brought me to the point of looking for a collaborator, of turning the idea into a reality? Like any good psychiatrist, I need to go back to when I was young. I remember as a child trying to understand the why and how of people's behaviour around me; it was my way of coming to terms with the inconsistencies that I experienced in family life. My own enlightenment and self-discovery were the main, if not the most readily acknowledged, motivation for entering the world of psychiatry and psychotherapy. I began by taking myself off to university where I studied psychology. Psychology is not, as many suppose, a discipline that teaches you to look inside people's heads and know what they are thinking. It is a wide field that takes in everything from linguistics through social psychology to the chemistry of the brain. Following this I went to medical school, became a doctor and trained in the speciality of psychiatry. A short sentence that took about ten years. Since entering psychiatry my passion has been for psychotherapy and, although it is hard to say when my training began, I'm certain it is a journey that will never end. Much of what follows comes from what the groups, individuals and families have taught me as I have tried to assist them in their own struggles.

One of the most important things that I have learnt of so far is the existence and power of the unconscious. I have become convinced that if we wish to discover our true selves we must allow our unconscious feelings, impulses and desires to surface into everyday awareness. If that sounds a dubious, unintelligible or even blasphemous claim then I hope this book goes some way to justify it. For those who are interested, my theoretical roots are planted in the teachings of Sigmund Freud and in the insights of those who have sought, with integrity, to build upon them. What, you may ask, has all this done to my Christian journey? Good question. I think that in recent years I have lost touch with a sense of mystery and simple faith. In learning to explain so much of what I see and feel I have eclipsed within myself the parts which do not readily subject themselves to psychological reason. One of the pleasures of writing a book in dialogue form is the relationship that inevitably springs up in such a shared experience; it is the result of sharing knowledge, exploring new ideas and comparing different points of view. The material in this book and the relationship that made it possible are part of my journey away from the eclipsing illusion of my own omnipotence and towards the reality of wisdom and gentleness. My hope is that our conversations will be a faithful companion to others on the same journey. After all, if we seek to learn about ourselves and each other, to develop our judgment and examine our motives, we cannot but become more wise and gentle. And an environment of gentleness, both within ourselves and shared with others, is the best one in which to live and mature.

Richard Christians are amphibious creatures and so are the churches to which they belong: they live in two dimensions. There is the dimension of the spirit. We believe that we are not alone in the universe, that there is a dimension to reality that we call spiritual; though it interpenetrates this reality, it has its own integrity. It is difficult to describe this amphibious experience, though the language of dimensionality may help. We are very used to thinking of reality as three-dimensional and time as linear, but modern scientific studies, especially in quantum physics, now show that the universe is much more mysterious than our previous picture allowed us to believe. There may well be dimensions to reality that we cannot yet comprehend, whole areas of experience that we have shut ourselves off from, or have lost the capacity to relate to. It is similar to the way a colour-blind or tone-deaf person is unable to appreciate certain works of art or pieces of music.

I'm not meaning to be argumentative in this introduction but I do want to make certain assumptions on behalf of Christian believers. The main assumption is that there is more to reality than the conventional view today apparently admits. Christians believe in the reality of God and in the fact of encounter with God; they believe in the reality of the spirit and in the energy of that reality. The energy of the spirit, as I have already implied, interpenetrates and infuses this reality. It is not separate from it, not a department of it, not a compartment of life. Dylan Thomas captured something of what I am trying to say when he talked about 'The force that through the green fuse drives the flower'. This is why versions of Christianity that try to carve out a holy area, spiritual sphere or religious department in life are deeply mistaken. God's creative love undergirds, upholds and penetrates everything, it is not to be thought of as inhabiting a religious department somewhere. A possible illustration might be a university that contains many faculties, including arts, science, languages and theology or religious studies. If the universe is like that university it is improper to think of God as occupying only the divinity faculty. The universe as a whole is the sphere of God's gracious concern and nothing is alien to the divine love.

Nevertheless, one of the ways human beings have to operate is by an economy of concentration, and this can easily lead to compartmentalization. For instance, in order to affirm that all days are holy, that all time is God's time, we set aside one day to celebrate the fact. We are told in Scripture that there is no temple in heaven. Presumably the sense of God's reality will be direct and all-embracing and no longer necessitate particular application or concentration. In this life, however, distractible creatures that we are, we divide and concentrate in order to do justice to important realities. One of the functions of the Church is to help us do that, to witness to the universality of God and to invite us, however infrequently, to recollect it, to be aware of it and, indeed, to attend to it. Amphibious Christians acknowledge that, for whatever reason, the pressures of time and material reality, themselves the work of God's hands, can so absorb us that we can fail to ask their meaning or remind ourselves of their origin. By the same token, it is possible by an act of absent-mindedness or sheer wilfulness to cut ourselves off from the energy of God and the world of the spirit. This happens to me all the time; but there was a period in my life when it happened in a very radical way.

About five years after I was ordained I completely lost faith in God and was, to all intents and purposes, an atheist, a deeply troubled atheist but an atheist nevertheless, or so I felt. I had lost all sense of the reality of God, the presence of God, the meaning of God, the existence of God. For any believer this would be a distressing experience. It is particularly difficult for an ordained minister who is, as it were, a professional believer who lives by the Gospel and is supported by the Church. I was on the point of leaving the ministry and the Church when I came down with flu. The flu was followed by a period of convalescence in which I was clearly in some kind of depression. I was in this state for two weeks. I remember turning back to music and poetry and certain theologians that I had cut myself off from. Gradually the tide ran in again and I found myself slowly returning to faith, rather the way a plant which hasn't been watered slowly revives when given a good dousing. I realized that I had been cutting myself off from whole dimensions of experience. I had been starving myself of spirit. I had turned my attention elsewhere, turned my back upon sources of spiritual intimacy and refused to take spiritual nourishment. It is hardly surprising that what little faith I had withered almost to extinction. Things have not always been rosy since then, of course. I continue to repeat the same experience, though never so radically, and I always recognize the symptoms: a reluctance to pray, a longing to surrender myself to God in prayer, accompanied by a strange, almost sulky, inertia. The parallel that suggests itself is the breakdown in intimate relationships between husband and wife, or parent and child, where we know that we must make up, and won't be happy until we restore the relationship. But some spring of negativity or contrariness delays the gesture, the turning back to the other, the opening of oneself again to the risks of love.

So, being a Christian is an inexact and risky thing. We live very much in the world and are affected by its culture, its pressures, its fashions and fanaticisms. We also live in the world of the spirit and seek to open ourselves to its gracious and transforming power. We are, therefore, amphibians and the Church reflects this duality. It is both human and divine, the place where we encounter God, and also very much the place where we encounter one another in all our flawed humanity. This book has grown out of a fascination with the way Christians allow their humanity to intrude upon and impede the interpenetration of the Church by the Spirit of God. Anyone

who has been into a church or around churches for some time
will soon recognize that, like other human institutions, they
can be cockpits of conflict; deeply neurotic places where people
play power games and deny the reality of their own
circumstances. I have witnessed these things and been part of
the strange collusion that allows churches to be extremely
dishonest places. Yet they are also places of encounter,
witnesses to the reality of God, the sign that tells hurrying
people that there may be more to life than they allow
themselves time for. I've always been very moved by the words
of a Roman Catholic priest who lived in a teeming slum and
worked at a dead-end job in a local factory. He lived the life of
anonymous Christianity. When asked why he did it he said that
he was there to keep the rumour of God alive in that place.
Churches serve the same function; indeed, we could put it more
robustly by saying that they serve as places of encounter with
the living God, places of grace, healing and forgiveness. In my
own experience I have been hurt, exasperated and
misunderstood in the Church, but I have also been deeply
ministered to. I have received the inexpressible grace of
forgiveness and love; I have been understood and accepted as I
am. The Church has mediated grace to me.

In these pages, however, we will be taking much of that for
granted and concentrating, I hope not perversely, on the way the
Church impedes that ministry of grace. In this conversation we
shall be focusing on the ways in which we allow ourselves to
stifle the spirit and impede the work of grace. Thank God that
we can never cut it off entirely. It seems particularly
appropriate that this is a conversation between a church leader
and a psychiatrist who is also a Christian, but who has a
bracingly realistic approach to Christianity and his own part
in it. Speaking personally, I have learned much in the exercise
of my pastoral ministry from the insights of psychologists,
psychiatrists and psychotherapists and their approaches to

human unhappiness and sinfulness. Without making too many claims for them, they have offered the people of our century priceless insights into the complexities of human nature and the way we are wounded by life, particularly by our early experiences, and how we carry these scars with us to the grave. It is God's longing and desire to heal us and offer his power to transform us. In the Church this happens in many ways, but God is a God of nature and while miracles do occur which appear to short-circuit normal processes and developments, the more usual experience of Christians is that they are slowly loved and guided into maturity. Our part is to cooperate with the Spirit of God and acknowledge the truth of our own condition. The only real tragedy in life is to deny reality, the reality of our own nature and the reality of God's saving love. The Scottish theologian John MacQuarrie reminds us that reality is another name for God. If we run from reality and truth, we run from God; but if we face up to reality and no longer deny it, we will find a gracious and accepting power. In this conversation I have brought my intimate personal and theological knowledge to a young psychiatrist, whose insights and penetrating analysis of the ways in which we interrupt God's transforming love have helped me to understand the human predicament more clearly, find hope in dealing with it, and consider strategies for going beyond it. I hope that readers, even if they do not agree with everything they find in this book, or are made uncomfortable by parts of it, will recognize that it is a work of love that is offered to people to help them understand the springs of their own actions as well as the good and bad ways that things happen in the Church.

Most People Have a Problem With Church

People Have a Problem With Christians

Richard As a Christian, albeit sometimes an uncomfortable Christian, I often find myself more at home with what I would think of as healthy-minded unbelievers than with certain kinds of believers. I often find myself more accepted - they are accepting me as I am.

Brice There's no undercurrent of judgment?

Richard That's right. I mean, I know myself to be lacking in many ways, but I find certain kinds of Christians make me feel more wanting in something, whereas often with a very happy secular person who has no heavy religious agenda I feel, in a paradoxical way, accepted completely - in a way that mirrors what I think I get from God. The bottom line for me is that I am loved and understood in my fallenness, my brokenness, my lack of development, my humanness.

Brice Are you wondering why you sometimes feel more accepted by non-Christians than by Christians?

Richard Yes, exactly. Now, what is that about?

Brice Well, I think what it is partly about is a very popular and little-recognized human foible called 'projection'. Projection is an unconscious process by which we attribute to another person thoughts or feelings that are actually our own. This has the effect of making the original feelings more acceptable to us. For example, someone who dislikes a colleague may impute feelings of anger and dislike to him. In this way, his own feelings of dislike may appear justified and become less distressing.

Richard You say it's an unconscious process – that means that we don't realize we are doing it?

Brice Exactly.

Richard But what do we gain by projection? There must be a payoff.

Brice There are two short-term gains which drive us to project but ultimately they backfire and leave us worse off. First, by giving someone a recognizable, if inaccurate, identity we turn them into a known quantity and so make ourselves feel safer – they fit into our world-view. And secondly it gives us a chance to project or throw in front of ourselves, on to the other person, those things that we would rather pretend weren't part of us.

Richard Things like a sense of guilt, anger, hypocrisy, unholiness and despair?

Brice Yes, and it makes us free to disapprove of all the things that person now represents which we dislike and have learnt to deny the existence of in ourselves.

Richard So the people who make me feel judged are getting a relief from their own unbearable sense of guiltiness by foisting it off onto me, even though they probably don't know they are doing it and I obligingly start taking their feelings on to myself?

Brice Exactly, it is an 'unconscious' process; it happens without us realizing it . . . Until now anyway. The danger is that you might go away thinking that the feeling you have is really yours and start living out a misery that is someone else's. Then, to get relief, you project it into someone else and so on. Before you know it, everyone in the church is wallowing in a bog of guilt and judgment. Remember, though, that this thing is double-edged. You might be projecting your own judgmentalism into these people because you can't face it in yourself. In other words, what you are complaining about in them might be your own stuff looking back at you. Nasty.

Richard Okay, I've taken that on board. Referring back now to my original situation, when a newcomer or a visitor comes along will they get sucked in, exactly as I described it before?

Brice Probably, and if they don't join in with what's going on they get spewed out again as beyond hope: too wicked for redemption. There's something else; imagine what happens if the newcomer is the new minister.

Richard What a thing to inherit. Could it be that the previous incumbent was partly responsible for the mess?

Brice Definitely. I'm afraid a great deal of destructive projection comes from the pulpit, thinly disguised as the Word of God. But you must remember that it takes two to tango. We are all partly responsible when things go wrong so we must accept responsibility for trying to put them right. Which I suppose is what this book is about.

Richard Is all projection bad and destructive?

Brice No, we can give other people good bits of ourselves, but we should only loan them; we need them back and they have to find their own good bits.

Richard What about no projection at all?

Brice You've probably met more really holy people than I have. You know, folk who are content and know they are loved by God. Not passive or wet, but not needing to project stuff either. The company of these people is intoxicating but troubling as well.

Richard They aren't available for projection and so you have to live with yourself?

Brice Precisely. Like I say, troubling . . . Let's move on.

Richard Okay . . . So there I am, visiting a church, talking to someone - it might even be the minister - and during the conversation, which by the sound of it might be rather one-way, I start feeling things I'm not used to and thinking things about myself that aren't familiar. What do I do then?

Brice Well, if you are like most people, you are likely to mistake the uncomfortable things you are feeling for your own and drift away, believing God thinks you're a louse.

Richard What could I try to do instead, Doc?

Brice That's harder. You need to be able to tell the difference between your own feelings, hang-ups, madnesses and good bits, and those of others. As you learn to do that, and most people are better at it than they think, you will find yourself becoming angry when you notice someone using you as a garbage dump.

Richard That makes sense, but I expect people will find it hard to accept that anger will help in this situation.

Brice I'm sure you're right. But that's because most of us, Christians in particular, are taught to despise and deny our angry feelings. This is a pity because anger is a simple emotion that tells us when something is wrong. Unfortunately it gets lumped together with rage and hatred and we are all a little afraid of it.

Richard And you think our fear of anger stops us being honest with each other when it counts?

Brice It's certainly part of the story. We'll be coming back to it.

Psychology and Religion

Richard I want to ask you what you think the relationship is between psychology and religion. From the sort of things you've been saying, it's obvious you think there is one.

Brice Yes I do, but it's complicated and I'm only beginning to understand it.

Richard So you can't answer my question?

Brice   No, and I'd be foolish to try. I could make a few introductory observations instead. Would that help?

Richard   It would. Observe away.

Brice   Many people feel uneasy when they think of spirituality and psychological understanding as in some way related. Something tells us that the two are somehow in competition rather than, say, complementary. The New Psychology of this century feels, to many, like an attack on spiritual mystery. It was the same for the theory of evolution which was, and for some still is, seen as an attack on Genesis. Changes in social functioning are often pointed at as evidence of the undermining effect that psychology has had on Christianity.

Richard   Do you mean things like the possible link between our increasingly non-church-based culture and the mushrooming of psychological theories in recent years?

Brice   That's right. It is easy to assume that they are somehow linked, the one is destroying the other. It won't surprise you to learn that I think there *is* a link but that it is not the obvious one.

Richard   You're right, it doesn't. What is it?

Brice   I'll explain, with squirrels . . .

Richard   Seems logical . . .

Brice   Everyone knows that the grey squirrel drove the red squirrel out of England and that's why it is almost completely confined to Scotland.

Richard I'd heard that somewhere.

Brice You may be interested to know that it's not true. The grey did not actually *drive* the red out. People simply assume this because the grey now lives where the red used to. The truth of the matter is that man disrupted the shy red squirrel's habitat to such an extent that its numbers dwindled right away south of the border. The new habitat: different trees, parkland, more urban areas, that sort of thing, happened to suit the grey very well, so it moved in and colonized. The grey saw an opportunity and it took it.

Richard And you think it's the same with psychology and religion?

Brice Yes. Churches and their message have become increasingly less relevant to people so they have cast around for something else to feed the ache. Some of the racier versions of the new psychologies have met that need. Back to the squirrels. It is the similarities between the squirrels that make it appear as if they are in competition with one another.

Richard And the same goes for psychology and religion?

Brice I think so, yes. It is tempting to think that psychology has driven out religion. I can't prove it, but I think that where the two meet, they are, in fact, responding to the same thing: the hope that there is something more to life. I'm describing what I've heard you call the religious impulse, the urge to mature.

Richard Assuming that what you've said has some truth in it, what *are* the similarities?

Brice   One is that the experience of either psychoanalysis or religion can bring about profound personal changes in people. I mean deep lasting change for the better here, not superficial adjustment to life's vicissitudes. Another similarity is a more shameful and telling one.

Richard   What is it?

Brice   That adherents to each approach are often just that. Adherents. They stick to their perspective like glue. Disparaging, inflexible, narrow, intolerant and complacent are a few of the adjectives that leap to mind to describe how we behave when we refuse to explore beyond our basic dogma. We are afraid to look left or right for fear of losing our way. We are like a certain kind of hill walker. We spend the whole journey up thinking about the top and the whole journey down thinking about the car park or the traffic on the way home. We only look at the view to gauge our height, and the marvels of nature all around us are only so much hindrance. Brain dead in paradise is, I think, an apt description of this state.

Richard   You sound like you've been there.

Brice   Oh yes indeed.

Richard   Are there any differences between psychology and religion that you want to mention before we move on?

Brice   Just one. For me, Christianity is the only route that will take me on my journey from the very beginning to the very end. Psychological understanding can't do this. What it can do is to help me along the way. For me it is a very important component of my journey.

Richard   What about the rest of us?

Brice   Decide for yourself, it's your journey. The thing it all hinges on is whether or not you believe in the supernatural. If you don't believe the Holy Spirit works in our hearts and minds and in the world, then for you there may be no real difference between the science of psychodynamics and the mystery of God.

Richard   It's a help to know where you stand. What do you say to people who think that you and your like are priests of a cult of the individual?

Brice   As is so often the case with criticism, there is some truth at the heart of this accusation. There are plenty of Christians, myself included, who sometimes use the rational basis of psychological understanding as a hiding place from the mysteries of God. But that doesn't mean that it is *meant* to be a hiding place; I'm misusing it. Living with psychological understanding in a Christian context is a risky business but we lose a lot if we chuck it out just because it's dangerous. It's like fire, it can be servant or master.

Richard   The reply I would give is that the New Testament, in comparison to the Old Testament *is*, at least in part, focused on the individual. But not at the expense of everything else. It's all about balance. Indeed, this dialogue is a practical exercise in that balance, in the relationship we've been talking about: a theologian talking with a psychiatrist about a common interest in Christianity and the Church.

Brice   As you say, something that we have in common is that we both got turned on to church rather than turned off. What drew you in to begin with?

Richard It was beauty that converted me. I was converted by
the beauty of God. That's what got me into church long before
I knew anything at all about theology, evangelism or even
Christian morality. I was taken out of the backstreets of a small
West of Scotland town by the local rector. He'd taken this small
industrial town church right up the candle, he'd made it into a
kind of Anglo-Catholic shrine. I walked in and fell for it. It
appealed to something deep inside me and I was instantly
committed. The aesthetic thing was obviously very important
to me, and it always has been, though not, I hope, in an
idolatrous way.

Brice I'm intrigued that you add that about idolatry. Do you
expect to have to explain yourself?

Richard One comes across people who suspect all the senses
except the sense of hearing; they think it is somehow
miraculously conceived and is, therefore, not distortable as a
way of being in touch with God. But, for these people, the senses
of smell and sight are highly suspicious and not to be trusted,
so they go in for a severe suppression of them. In this context
church buildings can end up as simply auditoria for golden
oratory. Avid listening, but nothing to look at or smell or touch.
Now, before this turns into 'On the psychiatrist's couch', I'm
going to turn the tables and ask you the same thing.

Brice It was simplicity that converted me. I was twelve at the
time and on a Scripture Union house party. These were holiday
camps where you did all sorts of sporting activities and each
morning and evening someone would get up and explain the
Gospel. It used to be called Muscular Christianity.

Richard Where does simplicity come in?

Brice The way the Gospel was presented was very simple: we've all sinned, the world's in a muddle but Jesus came on a rescue mission, here are the verses that show it. God offers you a choice: you can believe or not believe, the only way to really validate the claims are by your own experience. It was a call to faith.

Richard And you took it?

Brice Yes, I was a twelve-year-old looking for meaning and I found it.

Richard And have things been simple ever since?

Brice No, of course not, but it was a great start.

What Puts People Off Church?

Richard I'm fascinated by what puts people off church in the first place. Something happened to me the other day which I think fits in here. My son lives out in a farm cottage in the country. Some neighbours moved in a couple of months ago and he's got to know them. I popped in to see him one Sunday afternoon. I'd been doing a church service, so I had a dog collar on, and his neighbour introduced me to her young son who was obviously very puzzled as to who I was, this family having had no contact with the Church before. The little boy asked 'Who is that man? What is Mark's father?' and his mother replied 'Oh, he's a church man'. 'What does that mean?' 'It means you have to mind your Ps and Qs'.

Brice So here's a woman with little previous direct church experience who has nevertheless picked up that the Church is a cultural institution that stands for doing guilt things on people.

Richard And that's dreadful, because the bottom line in Christianity is exactly the opposite of what it apparently seemed to be for that woman and what it now looks like in so much church life. The most radical thing that Jesus talked about was total acceptance. 'Come unto me all ye that travail and are heavy laden'. 'I came to call sinners, not the righteous'. Something went terribly wrong when we moralized the faith.

Brice Explain please.

Richard Churches take a wrong turn when they get all tied up with ways of behaving, with ways of being perfect and good; whereas the thing that really marks out Christianity is that it is about God's gift to us. It is about God giving us grace, forgiveness and acceptance, like totally accepting parents. Obviously totally accepting parents want their children to grow up and mature; but their moral evolution is not what earns their parents' affection. Their affection is a given thing. It is not conditional on anything. It is unconditional love. This usually gets turned around by Christians into 'how can we so live that we can earn God's love?' This puts a premium on good behaviour, or, much worse, on appearing to behave well. As the writer Voltaire put it, 'Hypocrisy is the homage that vice pays to virtue'. You're not good but you kid-on that you're good. And you get disproportionately incensed with people who are being ostentatiously indifferent to these things.

Brice Okay, I understand now, but what I also see is that in a church where this is going on there will be a strong cultural pressure on every member to take part in the group hypocrisies.

Richard Indeed, and I think we will have much more to say about this later on, but it is worth noting that this is the opposite of what Jesus is about; he had it in for the hypocrites of the time, the Pharisees.

Brice And he opposed their destructive projection of their own hidden shortcomings into others. Instead, he preached that everyone is equal before God. No wonder they hated him so much.

Richard One of the problems with religious set-ups is that they are, to outsiders at least, very good at denying these sort of problems. Pretending things are all right when they are not. As a shrink you must come across this a lot. Have you noticed it in churches?

Brice Oh yes. In the church context there is sometimes a huge consciousness-raising job to be done just to get people to realize that they *are* uncomfortable about things. It is as if certain feelings and senses have been turned off. That's what makes newcomers and outsiders so valuable, they see the hypocrisies. Trouble is, it can also be a source of disillusionment for them. We are often quite poor at confronting painful issues.

Richard Expand on that a bit.

Brice I know that elsewhere you have described the Church as a truth-seekers' conflict zone and that is how it should be. But I wonder how much of that conflict is honestly aimed at finding the truth about things. For instance, disagreement often seems to result in schism, but schism is not necessarily what you'd expect if the conflict were genuinely part of a mutual exploration.

Richard You've got a point there. It's certainly true that there are over thirty thousand denominations worldwide. They reckon there's one born every day in the United States and there are all sorts of cracks about it. One of the stories I like is about some strangers who moved into a Scottish town. They asked the local elder how many churches there were and he replied, 'There used to be two but we had a union, so now there are three'. I think if people approach Christianity naïvely expecting a level of perfection and uniform holiness that you don't find, say, in a political party, then they are in for a very big disillusioning process. The clergy are often at the centre of that process. They are made to feel responsible for it. We are seen to represent God and we are a target for people's disappointment and disillusionment.

Brice But isn't there a game going on here? It's called 'You Failed Me So I'm Leaving'. It's what happens when people feel let down by churches for not being what they expected. They attack them for not being what they can't be anyway; perfect places to meet God. They leave disillusioned. The pay-off, for some disillusioned folk, is an almighty sulk. It's a shame if it lasts for the rest of their lives.

Richard Sometimes churches encourage this game by promising to be the perfect answer to life's questions. People who fall by the wayside are made to feel that it is because of their own shortcomings. Of course, it sometimes is.

Brice I've a lot of sympathy for those abused and disillusioned in this way. It takes a great deal of courage to have another go, to enter a church again. People, understandably, become very defensive.

Richard Defence is a very important element in the human game, isn't it?

Brice   Absolutely. Defences are fundamental to understanding the whole way we function, or more accurately, dysfunction. They are more than just 'being defensive' which we know as blustering and avoiding things. Defences proper run much deeper.

Richard   Before we go on, explain what you mean. I think the word 'defence' means something special to you psychiatric types.

Brice   That's right. We talk a good deal about defences or, more accurately, defence mechanisms. Everyone has them. They're an automatic, unconscious way of warding off the things we can't cope with. When our defence mechanisms go into action we don't notice it happening at the time – though we may realize later – what we were up to. Here are a few examples, complete with the names we psycho geezers give them. 'Repression' is the exclusion from awareness of impulses, emotions and memories that would cause distress if allowed to enter consciousness. For example, a memory of a humiliating event may be repressed. 'Denial' is closely related to repression. We infer that it's happening when a person behaves as if unaware of something that is obvious to others by, for instance, holding a belief that is contradictory to common sense. Some think that Christians live with a lot of denial of reality. Projection, which we have already considered, is a defence mechanism and there's another one we call 'reaction formation'. Reaction formation is what we call it when someone unconsciously chooses to behave in a way which is the opposite of how, deep down, they really want to behave. For example, excessively prudish attitudes to the mention of sex in conversation, or the media, may occur in someone who has strong sexual drives that they cannot consciously accept. So that's a few defence mechanisms. Plenty more where they came from.

Richard   That's a help, but where do we go with this sort of knowledge?

Brice   Everybody has a life story and it can be told in terms of our defences, and the defences of those who brought us up. The exciting thing is, and this is where our paths meet so exactly, that the future is not set, the story can be rewritten. We can change the script in fundamental ways if we can find the security to reflect upon who we are and who we are not.

Richard   If churches could somehow enable themselves to do that they could become redemptive agencies. I heard a poem recently and I found it quite liberating. It started: 'You don't have to be good . . .' and the thesis of the poem was that you can't start anything by being good at it. If you have it ingrained in you that you have to be good then you are going to be carrying an unbearable burden. I think everyone's lumbered with perfection. In espousing virtue and moral development the Church has somehow drummed it into people that they have to be mature before their time. If we could somehow turn the whole thing round and get people to see that this is a colossal field of development and adventure, then we'd be getting somewhere. Of course there are goals and aspirations: we are aiming to be virtuous and adult and mature, but we all start at different places of brokenness and incompleteness.

Brice   And it's okay to be like that?

Richard   Very much okay but, instead, we get locked into our own narrow and underdeveloped state when the whole purpose of Christianity is to move from that narrowness into abundance.

Some Baggage We Bring

Brice   Can you tell me what the word 'church' actually means in a way that doesn't leave me feeling confused?

Richard   I can try. Perhaps the best way into an understanding of the word is to link it to words that we do understand and one is the word 'election'. When you elect an MP you are choosing the person you want to represent you. A related word is 'eclectic'. People talk about an 'eclectic congregation' and that's not a parish church or a neighbourhood church, as such, but a place you choose to go to. Behind those words there's a Greek word which gives us the word for church and that is *ecclesia*. It really means 'the chosen people', if you like, those called out by God for a special function. There is also a human side to it: a church is made up of the ones who have chosen to follow Christ. So, putting it all together, I would describe the Church as a group of the chosen. These are people who have felt impelled by a particular vision or loyalty to Jesus or a way of following Jesus and have individually chosen to become a part of the community that contains and maintains the memory of Jesus.

Brice   By your definition a political party, for instance, can be a church inasmuch as it centres on a belief, a loyalty, a person, or all three.

Richard   That's right. You'll often hear politicians talking of their parties as churches. The Tory Party and the Labour Party would be correctly described as broad churches and the Socialist Workers' Party as a narrow church or sect.

Brice   Churches, and the people who go to them, are portrayed in a very stereotyped way. I guess it makes them more manageable. Can you avoid this trap and still describe the sort of people you come across? I think you are well positioned to take an overview. Start with the clergy.

Richard   I always tend to think that the clergy come in three types. There are the angry, the prophetic and the laid-back types. Or, looking from a different angle, there are the ones that are not really fussed, they are using the Church as a sort of easy billet. Then there are the hyperactive types, the workaholic types who very often get ahead, and the avuncular, pastoral ones who tend to be very popular.

Brice   What about the congregations, what sort of people come to church?

Richard   Well, there's the kind of person who hangs around the rectory, you'll always get people like that. They sort of become part of the family and seem to find their identity by being in the know.

Brice   They've found an angle on authority.

Richard   Then there are the patronizing bossy ones. They are often powerful people outside the church, but sometimes they definitely are not. They hope that church will provide them with an opportunity to become powerful.

Brice   Do you think some clergy join up for the same reason?

Richard   I'm sure it often comes into it. Anyway, often these bossy types treat the clergy like puppets. Sometimes the clergy collude with this. I suppose it makes them feel safe. In the States some really powerful businessmen like to develop a sort of patronizing role in the church, with the priest as mascot. You get lesser versions of it here. They want the church run like a big corporation, you know, kick ass, move in, move out, that sort of thing. I think the clergy get quite bullied by these sort of people. It's difficult when we find ourselves the victims of other people's need for power.

Brice What other types do you get?

Richard The perfectly straightforward people who are on a pilgrimage of faith or those who want to be told what to do and think; the dependent type. And then there are those who like to see the humanity of the clergy because they suspect they are just as human as they are. They like a bit of self-revelation.

Brice What about different levels of attachment to the church? For instance those whose attachment is quite nominal?

Richard In a funny kind of way they are the people I feel most comfortable with. The most worldly, least religious ones that I was talking about earlier. And, of course, the very dedicated disciples are there too.

Brice Is there any kind of common thread that you can identify that runs through us all?

Richard One of the good things about church is that it is very often a place where people who admit their needs and are not running away and hiding from them, will come. That's why I'm fond of quoting the statement of the French religious and political author, Charles Peguy, that nobody understands Christianity better than the sinner. The sinner is at the heart of Christianity. People who have a sense of their own brokenness, need and woundedness. These are the ones that let Jesus love them. It was the self-righteous, the ones who were not in touch with their own brokenness with whom he was most impatient. The publicans and prostitutes, whose ideals did not correspond to the actuality of their lives, were the ones he warmed to. It was the ones who hypocritically thought they had it all sussed out that he had problems with.

Brice   Not surprising, really. Their defences were up: they were pushing him away. For the broken people the defences had failed, and they knew it. But there is more here. We must, surely, have compassion for the self-righteous and hypocritical because that's all of us at some time or another. We all push God away, no matter how broken or holy we are. This happens when we are more afraid of what we will lose than what we might gain from letting God near.

Richard   The Pharisees and the rich young ruler (Luke 18:18-25) are all biblical examples of this terrible human trap.

Brice   Right, that's a help, because I'm interested in what makes a church group different from any other group. Let me explain. I notice in church groups – and I think we had better decide that 'church' means 'Christian church' - I notice in church groups, both large and small, all the misunder-standings, upsets, stucknesses and hurts that I see in any secular setting. And this begs the question, 'If there is a living God who has a dynamic day-to-day influence on the Church and its people then is there anything different about it?'

Richard   Such as fewer misunderstandings, upsets, stuck-nesses and hurts?

Brice   Partly, but there's more. The fact is that there often isn't much difference. If you like, being in the presence of God mostly feels quite ordinary. Our expectation is that it should be all bells and whistles and miracles and flashing lights and when it isn't there is a tendency for us to try to manufacture them. To take a couple of examples. Some Christians try to live in a sort of blessed fantasy world in which nothing nasty or unexplainable ever happens and they deny any hurtful or destructive consequences which their actions may have for other people. They do this by devolving responsibility on to God or the Devil depending on the prejudice of the moment.

Richard I take it you don't approve.

Brice Well, when people form into churches and behave like this they leave a trail of human and spiritual wreckage: individuals terribly bruised by an encounter with Christianity. There is much more to be said about this and we will come back to it in the chapter 'The Power and the Glory'.

Richard You mentioned two examples. What is the other one?

Brice It is more subtle and widespread; in fact most of us are probably prey to it at times. It is a sort of despair, or rather a defence against despair.

Richard Right, I understand that. Now what is the despair about?

Brice I believe it to be a deep-down feeling that God is not real or that, if he is real, then he does not really love and accept us.

Richard And the unadmitted fear that the one we love might not be there, loving us back, makes us anxious and panicky and that is hard to tolerate.

Brice We then mount a defence to push down and replace the anxiety and despair. In this instance we deny it and repress it.

In Christian groups there are many different defences for this feeling, but the one I have in mind here is the whole process of institutionalizing our faith. It is possible to see churches working so hard on all the nuts and bolts of daily church life that it almost seems that there is a corporate fear that if they stop there might be silence, nothing. No God. To outsiders, of course, this all feels very suspicious and maybe, even without realizing it, they ask themselves why, if God is real to these people, they are so busy doing anything rather than get to know him.

Richard You're suggesting that, having sensed this defensiveness, they could be forgiven for going away thinking that Christians are a load of phoneys?

Brice I am indeed. And it's ironic, because if only the spell could be broken we might find it easier to admit our doubts and fears to each other and to ourselves. We might pause long enough to be more available to God.

Richard These two examples you have mentioned have in them important things that shouldn't be discarded. I'm thinking, on the one hand, of the ecstatic vision, the spiritual immediateness that is so evident in some of the more self-consciously Spirit-led churches (fulfilling, if you like, direct commands from the scriptures: 'Cast your cares on him', 'Seek first the kingdom of God', 'Come as little children'); and, on the other hand, of the necessity for organization and the inevitability that it will be imperfect.

Brice I think you're right. The problem is that any invitation to people in these extreme positions, and I think that might be most of us some of the time, can immediately be countered by reference to the justifying spiritual truth, or self-evident practical necessity, at its centre.

Richard 'My defences are there for a reason and woebetide anyone who comes crashing in to undermine them'. It seems as though we need our defences in order to function from day to day.

Brice Exactly, but there is a price to pay and that is that the castle built to keep things out also keeps you in. The shelter becomes the prison. In a church context, that means that congregations can become fierce defenders of their collective defences, with many rules (spoken or unspoken), protocols, prejudices and highly sophisticated, often rigorously justified systems for the ejection of members who waver from the group norm. The effect of this is to signal very clearly to the outsider what is expected of an insider and it puts off from joining those likely to rock the boat.

Richard I know what you mean. An example would be the rejection of a church member who falls foul of a moral stricture. This idea of defences helps to make sense of a lot of situations I come across.

Brice It is tempting to think that these things only happen in odd or fringe churches but they don't. They tend to be more obvious there, because of the black-and-white nature of the setup.

Richard The real danger areas are the ordinary middle-of-the-road institutions like, say, St Agatha's by the Gasworks.

Brice Where the process can be subtle and insidious, so much so that it is hard to believe it even happens.

Richard So, how do you know it does?

Brice Because I see people who have stopped growing emotionally and spiritually, churches that have stopped maturing, and people who feel abandoned by God and drift away.

Richard We will be coming back to this later on, but now I want to bring this discussion full circle and try to put it all together. We have seen how fear that God might not be real, despair that he might not love us, disappointment with the ordinariness of much Christian experience, and fear of disapproval by other Christians might lead us to become defensive as individuals or a church. Defences, by their very nature, are strongly held and inflexible, and become more so if they are challenged. What should I do if I visit a church or any other kind of group and find myself up against a defensive barrier?

Brice The first step you have already taken: observe the defence.

Richard I guess that isn't always very easy.

Brice Indeed. Just as with our old friend projection, you need to know yourself well enough to tell the difference between your own defences against, say, rejection or hostility, and those of the people around you. Otherwise the defences you see around you may actually be your own, being projected. The second step is to try to understand the hidden fear behind the defence and address yourself to that. If you can help dissolve away some of that, then the anxiety caused by it will be reduced and the need for the defensive activity removed.

Richard Can you give me a simple example?

Brice Of course I can; would I have put my head on the block without wearing a well-starched collar? I often get the pleasure of leading Bible-study and discussion groups with teenagers and other young people. Whatever the situation the start is the same: a circle of anxious people all clutching Bibles, notebooks and pens. Now, in the church background that I come from, the evangelical tradition, we set great store by regular daily Bible study and prayer. This is a terrible struggle for most of us, but such a fundamental aspect of our church culture's identity that it is seldom talked about openly or, if it is, it is only to send us on a guilt trip. To get to the point, what I do in this situation is to follow the steps I outlined above. First, I sense the anxiety and notice the defensive posture which says 'It's all right, I'm a serious Bible student and I probably pray a lot too'. Secondly, I wonder what the hidden fear is. In this situation, it is usually that people have got the message from somewhere that they will be rejected and humiliated if anyone finds out that they have been unable to study or pray for a while. They may even have the idea that God stops loving them if they don't manage to pray and study and they certainly don't want anyone telling them that.

Richard So it is a loaded situation. What do you do?

Brice It's always slightly different because one has to tailor one's intervention to the moment and also be honest and sincere. Last time this happened I didn't even open my Bible, I just pushed it away a little and said something like 'I don't know about you but I've had a hell of a week and found it really hard to find time or the inclination to pray. Does anyone else get like that?'

Richard What happened?

Brice   Well, because I had addressed myself to the hidden fear and not the defence ...

Richard   You hadn't given them a load of verses to scribble down.

Brice   Exactly. Because I had addressed myself to the hidden fear the anxiety went, the defence diminished and we spent two hours talking about who we really are and how much God loves us. When we did open our Bibles to study, it was with a will and a pleasure and not out of a grinding, despairing duty.

Richard   That seems to make sense as far as it goes, but it will have to stand up to wider application if it is to be of any use. As you've mentioned, I think that the Church is a truth-seekers' conflict zone, and rightly so; people who care enough about the truth are going to disagree. I want to consider the whole group and institution thing a bit more. The Church is less easy to manage than, say, a factory for making garden furniture. Churches are not just human groups organized round a straightforward task. They are primarily places of divine encounter, places where we wrestle with the meaning of God and the meaning of our own lives. They are bound to be untidy.

Brice   It is certainly true that churches are not good at handling chaos and conflict constructively. A mark of increasing maturity in the individual is the ability to manage inner conflicts and chaos in a way that promotes greater emotional stature. The key to large groups moving on is the emotional and spiritual health of the individuals within them.

Richard   Do you relate that to churches?

Brice   I do. I've known churches that get to a certain point in their maturity and then plateau out. They've forgotten their centre. If you forget the heart of a thing then, ultimately, everyone ends up not giving a damn.

Richard   What's next?

Brice   How about . . .

Things That Go Wrong When We Try to Mature

Richard   I want to ask you about frustration. People come to me and they are frustrated. They've tried this and that and life still seems to be grey and meaningless. They are bewildered. There is no point in anything.

Brice   I'll bet they are doing a lot of blaming as well.

Richard   Quite often, yes. It's mostly themselves they blame but often the church or God. Why do you ask? Do you think blame has something to do with frustration?

Brice   Yes, because blame is a blind alley. Watch children when something gets smashed, they all point at each other to escape the blame. Blame seems to restore everything to normal, but it doesn't because there is someone left carrying the can. Or, to take another example, when a small child tries to come to terms with the sudden death or absence of a parent, it will often blame itself. Self-blame is the only thing that seems to make any sense of things. 'I'm deep-down bad, that's why horrid things happen to me'. The next step to that is, 'I deserve to be unhappy, what else should I expect?' This is frustration of the soul and leaves

us feeling unable to do anything about our predicament. Some
people protest and struggle against this. They wrestle with life
- with other people - and try to squeeze a sense of meaning from
it. Others despair of relief from self-blame and frustration, they
turn their suffering inwards and try to pass through life
unnoticed. As the American writer and social critic Henry
Thoreau once said: 'The mass of men live lives of quiet
desperation'.

Richard   Always the same story. What we want is over there,
where we are is here and frustration is in between. What can
we do?

Brice   We must find a way of moving through self-blame into
taking responsibility. Only in that way will we work out what
is real to us and what is rubbish we don't need.

Richard   That's all very well, but it won't do.

Brice   Why not?

Richard   Because what you've described is a vicious circle.
When we are frustrated and despairing that's when we are least
equipped to help ourselves. It's no help for you to say that we
must.

Brice   That's quite true, but notice that I haven't said that we
are left to help ourselves. We are like the explorer who has a
map in one hand a piece of toast in the other but doesn't know
which is which. Does he eat the map and read the toast or the
other way round? These questions are, of course, meaningless
to him because he doesn't know which is which. Like so many
of us at different times in our lives he flops down and says to
himself, 'I don't understand. What don't I understand?'

Richard And that's frustration in a nutshell. We explorers need help.

Brice We need to understand this frustration thing a little better. Our defences are in place, as we've already found out, to protect us. This they do and often very well. But our defences can also become imprisoning; this is where the frustration is generated. Ultimately our defences frustrate our attempts to form deeper relationships. They frustrate us and they frustrate those who want to draw near to us. They defend us from our insecurities about relationships but greater security will only come from the experience of deeper relationships.

Richard More frustration.

Brice Very much so. Our defences keep us safe from harm about as well as they keep us safe from help. Giving them up is scary enough, it feels so vulnerable a process. But it also changes our self-identity, and that can be even more terrifying. Growing seriously threatens our notion of who we are. The good news is that what we are actually threatened with is letting go of what we are not in order to be what we are.

Richard I've heard this sort of thing before and some of it is very good. My problem with it is that it is good news for people who are at the very healthy end of the scale and bad news for the rest of us. It sounds like you're just loading us with more frustration. What you say is all very well in theory but in practice it simply doesn't help.

Brice You're right, which is why what is coming next is important. There is, as you imply, a trap for the unwary. It's a trap that many preachers and people in the growth industry fall into.

Richard   And it is?

Brice   Simply that the tools we need to open the safe are locked in the safe itself. Encouraging each other to somehow, magically, let go of our anxieties, our insecurities and our defences, is about as sensitive as inviting a headless man to a hat show. When people say to us that we must 'trust and let go in order to grow' they are only telling part of the story and they mock us to the core. They may not mean to, but that's what they are doing. We even do it to ourselves. We say to ourselves things like 'Tomorrow, I'm going to wake up and magically stop doing all these sinful things'. Now, I know that God works miracles in our hearts and minds - if there's any difference - but it's almost never instantaneous and nearly always with our participation or assent. We will save ourselves a lot of despair and disillusionment if we resist the temptation to behave thoughtlessly over this. To illustrate: every Sunday some preachers get up in the pulpit and exhort their congregations to be perfect by the next Sunday, or else. All they do is paralyse the gullible with guilt, enrage everyone else and parade their own inner despair for all to see.

Richard   And you think there are better answers to all this?

Brice   Possibly. I'm sure there are some better questions.

Richard   Such as?

Brice   Such as, what are the fears and desires that cause our insecurity in the first place? What are the things that we do to ourselves that perpetuate the frustration and the vicious circles? What are the ways we frustrate each other? How does God want to help us with this, and what stops me getting to the point of accepting his security? We need help with the answers to these questions. That's why the question to ask is not 'How can we help ourselves?' but 'How can we help each other?'

Richard And that, amongst other things, is what the church is for.

Brice Do you think it manages it?

Richard A lot of the time, yes. It's a muddle and a struggle at times but churches are about meeting together and trying to commune with God. I think churches do give us quite extraordinary possibilities for communion with God, but at the same time they are also very human. They are capable of the most terrible misjudgments and corruptions. Churches are also places where we can help one another to grow and mature in our faith. I would pitch my claim for the Church pretty high, yet also be quite realistic about it. At its best it is always very humanly muddled. Tell me how, exactly, we can help each other with our frustrations?

Brice It's all about relationships. And the pattern for that is the Gospel itself which offers us a relationship with God. This is endorsed in numerous ways in the Bible. Jesus constantly refers to our relationships with God and with each other. I think this is central to any mature understanding of church, but it is also fraught with human complications. The main complication is that our capacity to have nourishing and maturing relationships with others is directly related to the quality of our relationship with ourselves.

Richard You'll have to explain that. Convince me it's not psychobabble.

Brice If your relationship with yourself is generally good then your capacity to relate to others, to grow together, will also be good. If, on the other hand, our relationship with ourselves is poor, then we will find maturing with others difficult. Think of the commandment to love our neighbours as we love ourselves. Most of us keep this commandment better than we think. Most of us do love our neighbour in the same way we love ourselves. 'Poor neighbour', is all I can say. This commandment can also be seen as a promise: 'With my help', says God, 'you will be able to love your neighbour as you love yourself'.

Richard Our weakness is that we try to become what we think we should be. We try to be good in order to be accepted. Another frustrating dead end. Thank God that the Church is meant to be a place of healing.

Brice I agree, but it is not a place of *inevitable* healing. We have to take some responsibility for it. In any worthwhile relationship both parties take responsibility for the health of it. That goes for our relationship with God – Jesus' teaching faces us with many choices – and it goes for our relationships with each other.

Richard What sort of choices?

Brice We don't like it when the truth about something makes us uncomfortable. We deny it and get cross when we are reminded of it. If we are reminded often enough and in an environment which makes it safe enough to think about it, we move to acceptance. We realize that we only stand to lose things we don't need anyway. This can often take a long time and a lot of coaxing. Often we have to go through the painful process of, as it were, growing new ears. Ears that allow us to listen and aren't glorified bungs in the sides of our head: designed to block out upsetting sounds but now blocking out good things. It is just as well that God promises never to abandon us, to be ready when we are.

Richard We are children stumbling into the light.

Brice Well put. Let's look at this overused idea of acceptance a little more. We discussed how self-blame can be a dead end, in the same way guilt is a dead end unless we let it become shame. For it is only when we are ashamed that we will be able to ask for and accept forgiveness. Guilt does not drive us towards forgiveness for the simple reason that forgiveness is a communication in a healthy relationship. Guilt seeks a hiding place, it knows it is unloved. Shame and forgiveness re-establish and strengthen our relationship with God and each other. Repentance is closely linked with self-acceptance and is a terrifyingly vulnerable way to live. It is not just about saying sorry, it is about facing up to things as they really are.

Richard Being stuck, lonely and hidden, with feelings of guilt, is one of the most awful things I can think of. It's a kind of hell.

Brice God sent Jesus to coax us out of hiding and we have each other to help.

Richard That's what the Church is, each other and God. Before we end this chapter, I want to pin you down on something more. You're quite hot on this whole 'choice' thing. You say we have choices to make and yet I know, and I'm sure you do, that it's pretty hard to figure out what they are. What do you mean, exactly, by 'making a choice'?

Brice At the risk of vexing you further I'll try to show you what choice means for me with a story. I grew up in the country, I had a gun and I used to go shooting. One day I was walking through a defunct apple orchard when I saw that I was about twenty yards from an enormous wood pigeon. It made no attempt to fly off but simply regarded me, from a low branch, in an unruffled sort of a way. Without thinking I pulled the rifle up and took a bead on its neck (a neck shot is always impressive because it is a small target and leaves the carcass undamaged). As my finger squeezed the trigger, I imagined the admiration at home for a shot taken from fifty, maybe a hundred yards, whatever I thought I could get away with. I looked at the pigeon and it looked at me. It was vast, obviously old and seemed, the more I looked, to be rather venerable, almost wise. I did not shoot at it. Indeed, I was so fascinated that I lowered the gun and walked up to it. I saw that it was breathing very slowly and its eyelids were drooping. I realized that this great bird was dying of old age right in front of me. Slowly, with the back of my little finger, I stroked the soft feathers on its neck; a neck I had, moments before, meant to split open. Thinking about it now, I can see that by not trying to get away from me the pigeon had given me the opportunity, the choice, not to fire my adolescent cruelty down the barrel of the gun and into its defenceless body. Instead, we shared, as two creatures, some moments of peace and gentleness. Eventually I left it dozing on its branch and went quietly home. The choice I had made when I lowered my gun changed something inside me, and changed it for good. But notice this, the choice I made was not my first reaction to seeing the pigeon. My first reaction was to shoot it.

Institutions Obscure

What is the Church For?

Brice   Okay, an easy one to start with. What is the Church for?

Richard   The answer I like to that question is one that was greatly favoured by Catholic Anglicans for a long time. The Church was defined as the extension of the incarnation. The incarnation is the embodiment in flesh of God and that is Jesus, so we have to start by looking at the relationship between the Church and Jesus. The Church is the mechanism, either divinely inspired, or humanly constructed, or somewhere in between, it depends where you are coming from, that continues to celebrate, encounter and make contemporary the reality and memory of Jesus Christ. Now that's quite a complex phenomenon and we should try to unpack it in a variety of ways, but essentially it is about the continuing of the reality of Jesus in history.

Brice We don't really know much about Jesus, do we? I mean historically.

Richard That's right, although a great deal has been written about him. And even though within fifty or sixty years of his death we had the four gospels of Matthew, Mark, Luke and John as well as the letters of his first generation of followers, Peter, Paul and John, it would be a mistake to see the Bible as offering a biography of Jesus' life. We can, however, be reasonably certain about some things and what does seem to be sure is that Jesus was a teacher, a healer, a wandering holy man and a significant Jewish prophet. The Scriptures, as I've said, are not history books, but they contain historical material that we can make use of, especially if we couple them with secular records and contemporary histories by other authors. For instance, we can locate the time that Jesus was crucified by Pontius Pilate; that's the date stamp in the Christian Creed and it is put there precisely. Now we may not know whether Jesus was born of a virgin and we may not know quite what to make of the resurrection accounts, but we do know that a hullabaloo occurred in about the year 30 AD because this prophet was executed by the Romans at the request of the Temple establishment. We also know that he was a healer and a preacher who had a revolutionary approach to humankind's relationship to God: he wanted to create unmediated access to God. Jesus clearly wanted to break down the legal customs approach, the sort of uniformed branch idea that you could only get access to God if your passport was stamped by an official inspector.

Brice And replace it with a personal relationship with God, for everyone. I suppose knowing Jesus himself was the beginning of that.

Richard Yes, and that brings us on to the disciples of Jesus. They discovered that the only way they could describe or understand their relationship with Jesus was to understand it as an encounter with God. Jesus imaged God for them, expressed the divine mystery in accessible human form. We have to place a great deal of trust in their accounts of what happened and what they felt was going on. Certainly, Jesus created a band of followers and he seems to have had twelve of particular closeness called apostles, the Greek word for 'sent'; he sent them out to continue his message. He also attracted a group of women around him who looked after the temporal needs of both Jesus and his apostles. We know, for instance, that when he was crucified he was wearing a rather exquisite garment, woven throughout from top to bottom. This was so precious that the Roman soldiers didn't tear it up and divide it amongst themselves as was the custom. Instead they gambled for it. It is likely this cloak was made for him by his women followers. So we get a picture of a man who was loved and who created a community around him that, unusually for his day, included women and was threatened with dispersion at his crucifixion.

Brice And after the crucifixion?

Richard A few days after the crucifixion some event occurred that changed the lives of the people who had, for the most part, deserted him at the moment of his death. This was what we call the resurrection. Whatever happened, it turned them round from people who had deserted Jesus to people who now preached him as a new and abiding reality. The resurrection seems to be the 'big bang' that got the Christian movement going in history. From this point Christianity spread out into the world like galaxies into the universe.

The Christian Clubs

Brice   Before we go much further we are going to have to do a bit of spadework on some of the historical and technical, or perhaps theological would be a better word, aspects of the Church.

Richard   You mean we have to root ourselves in the whole collective experience that we call the Church so that we know where we are coming from?

Brice   Well, yes, seeing as you put it like that, I suppose I do. We need an overview of the various denominations in the Christian Church and I guess that's your department, isn't it?

Richard   Yes.

Brice   Off you go then.

Richard   As a very rough sort of shorthand I like to think of the Christian animal as coming in three basic species, each with their own particular approach. There is what I think of as the old Catholic understanding of Church and here I would include the Orthodox Church. This is one of the most fascinating, attractive and, certainly statistically, most powerful expressions of Christianity. There are more Roman Catholics in the world than any other kind of Christian and they claim continuity with the memory of Jesus from the very beginning. They claim to have been in continuous existence since Peter the Apostle.

Brice   What are the other species?

Richard   The other two species are the Reformed Churches and what I call the young Churches.

Brice Okay, I've got that. Now, I think there's more to say about the Catholic Church.

Richard Yes, there is. People of the Catholic Church type belong to an institution which is authoritative as well as authoritarian and as such offers a rock-like security. It is very self-confident in the claim it makes for itself: it alone is the true Church and the rest of us are somehow related to it. In fact that reminds me of an Anglican joke. One of my heroes of the faith, the writer Evelyn Underhill, was obsessed for years by the idea of becoming a Roman Catholic and she used to say that while the Anglican Church wasn't the city of God it was a respectable suburb thereof, so she stuck to it, being essentially a suburban type.

Brice The Catholics know where their roots are.

Richard And there is no doubt at all that the great thing that the Roman Catholics have going for them is this absolute self-confidence, this historic continuity. In many ways it is the only surviving absolute monarchy in history, and that is deeply attractive to many people. Its great virtues are obedience and absolute discipline. It really does generate holiness. Think of the number of nuns and monks there are in the world. Or think of the Jesuits. I visited El Salvador a few years ago and I was taken to the dormitory where a group of them had been massacred. Here Jesuits had been shot by the Salvadoran army, but it didn't extinguish an ounce of Jesuit opposition to the totalitarian regime in El Salvador. It was deeply humbling. This great monolithic, authoritarian Church, this old Church - although it constantly tries to renew itself - emphasizes one particular approach to Christianity: the absoluteness of the divine revelation. Obedience is its great virtue.

Brice   You make it sound very attractive. I expect that its flaws are the inevitable ones in a human institution where there are powerful and absolutist ideals coupled with a complicated human hierarchy. Individuals and groups might, knowingly or unconsciously, usurp the system for their own ends. They might feather their own nests or indulge in self-promotion.

Richard   That's certainly true, but it continues to draw a lot of people to itself and since all institutions are flawed anyway people think to themselves, 'Why not go for the solid virtues of this one?'

Brice   Okay, I've got that, what's next?

Richard   The Reformation. At the Reformation there was a sort of division between those content with the collective mystery of Rome and those who wanted more freedom to be critical and prophetic and individualistic. There was a tussle between what the theologian Paul Tillich calls 'the Protestant principle and the Catholic substance'. Both are very important, and they are best kept together, but the Church of that day could not bear them under the same roof.

Brice   The way you describe it, it sounds as though there was an opportunity for the Church to mature in a particular way but the human side of things broke apart.

Richard   Yes, there was a split in Christendom and the Protestant species resulted. The Protestant Church, at its simplest, can be thought of as a Church with an emphasis on the authority of the individual conscience; it is the authority of the reasoning intellect under God. Interestingly, it has created a rather middle-aged Church. You see, there is something venerable about Roman Catholicism in a way; there is even something attractive about being ancient. Protestant denominations on the whole tend to be rather grey, rather middle-aged and very worthy. They stand for solid Presbyterian virtues, they stand for self-respect and making a contribution and not being crushed monolithically, being democratic, all that. But there is something pretty uncharismatic about it. If you look at many of the middle-aged Protestant denominations at the moment you will see that they are struggling.

Brice   And the other species?

Richard   Around all that, dashing in and out, dazzling everyone with their brilliance and sometimes with their awful hang-ups are the young Churches. They are the new Churches, the charismatic, pentecostal, Bible-based fundamentalist Churches. They can be intensely authoritarian in a personal way, with people being told very precisely how to lead their lives, but they are also very techno-friendly. It is odd, really, because although they despite modernism, they make better use of high-tech than any of the other Churches. They don't buy into the modern psyche but they've got their fax machines all right.

Brice   And what identifies them particularly in spiritual terms?

Richard   They focus most of their sense of mystery and holiness on Scripture and tend to be literalist about that. This approach is attractively straightforward but it can cause all sorts of problems.

Brice   There's a great deal of information in what you've just outlined, but I think we have to be very candid about the fact that it represents nothing much more than a sort of fly-past of what's on offer.

Richard   Definitely – but, broadly speaking, the typology is not an inappropriate one: the venerable, the middle-aged and the young Churches. Of course there are lots of intersecting lines between them all, many subgroups and confusing inconsistencies; nevertheless I think it is a valuable way of laying out the conspectus of Christianity.

Brice   Fine. Let's move on to look at the way in which Churches regulate themselves.

Government and Authority

Brice   One way in which we can find out a lot about any organization is by asking how it governs itself. What is it like on the inside, in terms of authority, hierarchy and so on? We would usefully put another layer of paint on to our picture of the Churches if we were to consider this next. Bishops to kick off again I think.

Richard   Mmm . . . I would identify several government models in the various Churches. The basic one is the episcopal model and it is reasonable to think of it as the most primitive. There's a period up to the beginning of the second century when we are not sure how the early Church organized itself. The problem is that we can't reliably take our information from the New Testament because the terms they used in, say, the Acts of the Apostles don't necessarily mean what we mean by them today. The various writers talk about bishops and elders and deacons in the New Testament but we are not entirely sure that these characters had the same sort of roles as bishops and elders nowadays. However, by about one hundred and something a model of church government emerged that is what we call the threefold model: bishops, priests and deacons.

Brice And the bishops were the bosses?

Richard Exactly, they were the persons of unity around whom the church was administered and unified. They delegated their authority to priests, who were sometimes called elders or presbyters, and who were licensed, as it were, by the bishop to celebrate the Eucharist and to govern congregations. Further to this there was a kind of extra group called deacons. The word deacon means servant or, if you like, social worker. The model for this is in the Acts of the Apostles. The Apostles said to themselves, 'why are we wasting all this time handing out the soup to all these widows when we could be writing sermons and planning missionary journeys? Let's appoint deacons to do the soup.' So they did.

Brice And that's the basic structure is it?

Richard Yes, and so it remained for centuries. There are some who say that Jesus never intended to set up anything so elaborate. Probably they're right, but I suppose the Church had to organize itself. It was inevitable therefore that some bishops became more important than other bishops. For instance, if you were Bishop of Constantinople, you were going to be more important than the bishop on some muddy river away up in Asia Minor. The significant secular cities added a bit of clout. The point I'm getting to is that the pre-eminent city in the ancient world was Rome, and so the Bishop of Rome becomes a very significant figure.

Brice Is the link between St Peter and Rome important here?

Richard Oh, definitely. Almost certainly St Peter was martyred in Rome, as was St Paul, so there gradually developed a primacy associated with the Bishopric of Rome. This got tied up with the primacy that Peter undoubtedly had: Jesus called him the rock upon which the Church would be built. These two things helped to theologize Peter and, because he could be thought of as the first Bishop of Rome, his successors were thought to be of a special kind. Add to this the fact that the City of Rome was the secular centre of the world and we see very clearly the inevitability of the papal system where the Bishop of Rome was first of all first among equals.

Brice The equals being the other bishops?

Richard Yes. For although all bishops were supposedly equal you would go to the Bishop of Rome if you were having a dispute up the river in Asia Minor because only a senior wise guy got to be Bishop of Rome, so he got a name for sorting things out. Gradually this became formalized, so the papacy was formed. Soon a theology was developed that defined it and said, 'Yes, the Bishop of Rome is a distinctive and unique figure in Christendom'. There was a sense of the divine intent that this bishop should be first. This arrangement was basically unaltered up to the nineteenth century when there was a Vatican Council decree of papal infallibility whereby the Bishop of Rome becomes more than simply the most important bishop in the world; he becomes quasi-divine, infallible in certain modes.

Brice I get a real sense here of man, through this institution, albeit divinely inspired, stretching out to try and narrow the gap between himself and God. What confuses me slightly is that Jesus is portrayed in the Bible as God stretching out to us.

Richard The Catholics are very careful in the way that they define the Pope's infallibility. It is only when he is speaking very specifically in a certain mode that he is infallible. Nevertheless, there is a sense in which the Pope, the vicar of Christ, has an almost divine status and there is no doubt at all about the immense reverence and devotion that many Roman Catholics have towards him.

Brice So the papal system is a very heightened and pointed version of the episcopal system. Okay, forwards to the Reformation.

Richard At the Reformation there was a rejection of a whole way of understanding what the Church was. The idea that the Church could absolutely guarantee your post-mortem status or that you could actually buy entry to heaven, or time out of purgatory, by paying for Masses for the dead, was repugnant to the reformers. There was also a repudiation of the existing hierarchical system, and one of the main alternatives to it that evolved is the presbyterian system.

Brice I guess this one has a bit less of the vertical in it and rather more of the horizontal.

Richard It reckons that there has to be rulership and government in the Church but that it is too dangerous to give unprotected authority to a single individual. What has evolved is a kind of collegiate approach, what is called Presbyterianism. The governing body of the church is the local minister with his elders. They comprise the Kirk Session. The Kirk Sessions are replicated, on a grander scale, right on up to the General Assembly. So they end up with a system of checks and balances almost like the government of the United States where there are different houses that, in a sense, cancel each other out, or at least watch each other. It is a wonderful system in its way and very democratic, if you can call voting for who governs you democratic. The problem with this particular type of government, or polity, is that it is a bit cumbersome; it takes a long time to turn round. There are other polities of a more congregational sort where there isn't much of a concept of the Church as a global unit; the unit becomes the local congregation. These churches are, in a sense, private groups that run themselves, that loosely affiliate to one another and may even have assemblies and get-togethers.

Brice   Like the Congregationalists and the Baptists?

Richard   Yes, and on the whole, the unit of government is the local one. Then, of course, you get the new, more fringe, one-off polities where some guy will decide he has the answer and just jump up and start a church. Very often interesting things happen to those people – they can become very authoritarian, they call themselves the Apostle of the Age or whatever. Most of these people, interestingly, still try to peg the basis of their polity onto the New Testament in some way. But the thing about the New Testament is that it is more like an archaeological site than a blueprint. These people blow the dust off it and say, 'This is how they did things – we're going to replicate it.'

Brice   And because the Bible doesn't actually supply a blueprint of how to create a church they usually end up making most of it up and not really getting anywhere new.

Richard   That's right, except that I'd like to enter a note on the Anglican system. All church systems evolve, but the Anglican system, it seems to me, has evolved with particular rapidity this century. The Anglican Church retains the ancient episcopal system but it is no longer true to say that bishops govern the Church as once they did. The new element is the synodical system which brings bishops, other clergy and representative lay people into the government of the Church. Synod is the

Church's parliament. The recent decision to ordain women in the Church of England is a good example of its operation. In order for that decision to be taken each of the groups in the Synod, called houses, had to achieve a two-thirds majority. Whatever you make of it, the emergence of the synodical system in Anglicanism demonstrates that its organization is dynamic and evolutionary, not static. Right, I think that about wraps it up for a quick guide to the way in which the churches govern themselves.

Faith

Brice We've discussed, however briefly, what the Church is for, what flavours of church are on offer and how they govern themselves. Before we go on to talk about some of the ways in which things go wrong in our institutions let's talk about faith; the thing that keeps us Christians in our rather imperfect Churches.

Richard Let's take another strand from the definition that uses the Greek word for church, the root of our word for election. This gives us a picture of a group of people who have chosen to follow Jesus and, to some extent, have felt themselves called to follow him. Furthermore, this bunch of people claims to be having, however broadly interpreted, a living experience of the reality of Jesus.

Brice What you are describing is a sort of internalization - a taking in and making part of oneself - of the message and memory of Jesus. Words are inadequate to describe the process, but it is an experience that many seem to share.

Richard This is a large part of the essence of what a Christian is and yet a part that seems so thin and insubstantial to many who believe, or try to believe, and folly to many who look in from outside.

Brice I think it is sometimes hard to know when explanation is useless and must be abandoned to make room for mystery. Having said that I still want to ask you what makes believing so difficult?

Richard I suppose, if you were a very unbelieving person, then it would be the fact that Jesus has been dead and buried for nearly two thousand years. If you, for example, joined a group who claimed to materialize and make contemporary Abraham Lincoln or Robert Burns you'd be thought of by most people as nuts. Now when you go to a Burns supper you are having some kind of communion with the spirit of Burns through his poetry, but no one is actually claiming that Burns rose from the dead and is alive. But we do claim that Jesus is alive; after all, you see it on the side of buses: 'Jesus Lives'. Christians are making a distinctive claim: we are not just communing with the memory of Jesus, we are saying that through the Holy Spirit Jesus is encounterable by you and me. That is a claim that ultimately cannot be justified, it can only be experienced. One reason that people don't experience it is that the mediating instrument, through which the experience is offered, puts them off.

Brice By mediating instrument I presume you mean things like the context, the individual offering it, or the church institution embodying it. Sometimes these things or people are pretty off-putting or embarrassing.

Richard The mediating instrument can get in the way. Or it might be that a person, for whatever reason, cannot gain access to the experience. To some extent, though, entry into the Christian community involves abandoning something; it involves a leap of faith. The arguments will take you so far but there is what philosophers call a disjunction, there is a point where you have to say: 'Damn it, I'm going for it', and you have to make that leap. But it is a leap that is self-authenticating, it expresses and explains itself all at once. You can never actually see all the links in the chain that brings you from unbelief to belief because there is, oddly, always a link missing. It is hard to explain.

Brice For me, the same hand that holds on to belief also once held the unbelief. There is a tiny moment when my hand holds nothing and I know what it is to be unattached. There is something so deep down to do with a man or woman meeting God in that tiny moment, so defenceless and so unprotected, that it is not surprising that many individual Christian journeys keep coming back to it. Letting go of one thing to take hold of another is a major theme in the psychoanalytic world as well as the Christian one. There is something wonderfully, intensely human there.

Richard One of the images that I am fond of, and which makes this easier for me to grapple with, is of a stained-glass window in a church. If you come across a country church when you are out walking, you can't tell what the stained-glass window is like from the outside; you have to go inside and see the light pouring through it. It seems to me that this is how churches, in a baffled kind of way, have been explaining themselves for centuries. We don't argue from a start all the way to a conclusion. We can only bear witness to what we have seen and are experiencing and invite others to join us and see if something echoes inside them as well. And that does seem to go on happening. The Church goes on making its appeal, its challenge, in all sorts of different

ways and people go on responding. For some it's a kind of click
that goes in their minds, for others it is a kind of wistfulness;
they're not quite out and they're not quite in. When someone
encounters a Christian denomination, as well as encountering
all us mixed-up people, they are encountering Jesus.

Is The Church Human or Divine?

Brice What is fascinating is the way in which the Church, as
a large group of people with some sort of common aim, has
created institutions with rules and hierarchies many of which
are themselves not part of the recorded teaching of Jesus. They
came along later and we hope that they spring from the Spirit
of God in the Church. We have to trust that they do. I wonder
if it is reasonable to think of the different Churches as like
vessels afloat on a spiritual sea, the Spirit blowing in their
sails? You have already described some of the attempts to build
these vessels and, inevitably, because they involve people, they
are put together under tension, like the timbers on a ship. There
will be those who are part of the structure of this divinely-
inspired and divinely-driven institution who are not convinced
it is a reliable vessel or one fit for Jesus to inhabit. Nevertheless
they stick with it, joined in the common purpose.

Richard Until the tension gets too great and the vessel springs
apart, undergoes some sort of schism. Church history is full of
that. The Reformation being the obvious example. The thing is,
that it is an exponential process, as we saw earlier on: there are
thousands and thousands of churches all thinking to a greater
or lesser degree that they are the only reliable vessel for the
containment and promulgation of Jesus' memory and message.

Brice My limited knowledge of church history tells me that it is full of many different vessels afloat on this spiritual sea often taking pot-shots at each other, trying to sink each other or take each other over. What do you think is going on?

Richard Excitingly, something both very human, disastrously human at times, and also something deeply spiritual. Some of these large Christian groups which form Churches give the impression of great insecurity over their identity because they expend so much energy attacking the validity of other denominations.

Brice Nothing creates a sense of self-importance and identity in one group quicker than attacking another group. It isn't very healthy, but it *is* quick. We tend to be in a hurry when we are scared. You're in or you're out. The problem is that this activity can become an end in itself; it undermines the role of the Church.

Richard And yet with all these splits I think there is an honest if muddled attempt to rediscover the simple truths of the original message, to make things uncomplicated again. It is as if new churches come into being in an attempt to clear away some of the, essentially very human, overgrowth of the institution. This is most obvious when churches divide over single issues like baptism, or some aspect of their liturgy, or perhaps when one single tradition cannot contain two people with different views and powerful personalities.

Brice Isn't part of the problem here, that we get hung up on the outward trappings of our faith? We become, if you like, very style-conscious and outward-looking in an attempt to create the perfect vessel, the perfect church. Perhaps we have a need to distract ourselves from something less easy to grapple with and potentially more unsettling: the possibility that each of us

already has the purpose-designed vessel at our disposal anyway;
ourselves.

Richard   Sounds like you are suggesting that we don't need
churches?

Brice   No, I'm suggesting that our churches may sometimes
obscure the original plan by trying, albeit unconsciously, to
create an institution that is a substitute for a personal
experience of God. This might distract us from being available
to the inspiration of God, as individuals or as individual
members of large groups. There's a knife edge to be trodden here
and it is that, on the one hand churches can, often do, and are
at their best, when they point with all their wonderful
institutional paraphernalia at the divine, and at their worst
when with perhaps a tiny shift, they point with all their
wonderful institutional paraphernalia at themselves.

Richard   One of the most tragic aspects of the Church's failure
to mediate the presence of Jesus is directly to contradict it. This
is one of the most baffling things about Christianity. We are
grappling with the question of whether or not the Church is
human or divine; something we've made up or something from
God. In a strange kind of way we have to struggle with this one
all the time.

Brice   Go on.

Richard   We have to acknowledge that church, scripture,
sacrament and person are all instruments that the divine can
use. The technical expression in theological language is
mediating instrument; I used the expression earlier. They are
instruments through which the sound of the voice comes but
they are not the person who is making the sound. A primitive

response to a voice on the radio, reading solemn evensong out in London, would be to bow down and worship the radio. We are still capable of that kind of primitivism. In our churches we should have a proper kind of reverence for our mediating instruments but avoid idolatrizing them or worshipping them.

Brice The ideal being to hold our mediating instruments in place between man and God, but when we can't manage that, there is a risk that the stepping stone - the mediating instrument - becomes the journey's end. We get stuck on the messenger, be it icon or priest. Tell me, what is the effect in the church context of this kind of idolatrousness?

Richard The effect it has depends on the particular church culture. For instance, in the Anglo-Catholic culture there has developed around the celebration of the Holy Communion, the Eucharist, the Mass, the Lord's Supper, whatever you call it, a usage, a system, a ceremonial, a way of doing things . . .

Brice Before you go on, just explain what the Eucharist is . . .

Richard The word Eucharist comes from the Bible. It is from the verb 'to thank' and it reflects the fact that Jesus took bread and wine at the Last Supper and gave thanks for them, said grace over them. In the Eucharist we remember that event. For most Christian traditions the Eucharist is itself a mystery. It is experienced as a way of making Christ present now as a spiritual reality with which we can have communion.

Brice And a ceremonial system has developed around it.

Richard A ceremonial which presumably started as a very functional thing: a way of getting the bread and wine to the table; a couple of candles in a dark church without electricity;

everything would have its functional use. Then slowly that pure functionality changes, because one of the fascinating things about being human, and it is a lovely thing that we should celebrate, is that we have a genius for making the functional an end in itself. The thing that we do for one reason we continue to do for that reason but we also embellish and elaborate it, so because we have to move from A to B, each time we put a bit of a glide in and it becomes a dance step. We might want to project our voice to the other end of a large building and so we develop a chanting way of talking and shortly we've got music; we've got a chorus. We need spaces for worship so we build them and embellish them and soon we've got holy space, holy places. This is a wonderful, human elaborating instinct that we shouldn't be ashamed of. The problem begins, to go back to the original illustration of the ceremonial, when you start to fundamentalize that ceremonial. People start to say things like: 'You didn't move to the left of the altar by taking three steps, you took four. You made a mistake and you didn't bow in the right place either'. This way, the ritual, the thing that is meant to elaborate the worship and inform us, becomes an end in itself. Every Anglo-Catholic, every Roman Catholic has known people for whom the means has become the end.

Brice   Perhaps it's a sort of fear that if we don't build the temple right then the Spirit won't move. Perhaps paying too much attention to such things is a way, an unconscious way, of trying to nudge out the unpredictable, the divine.

Richard   In the church culture you are more used to, the evangelical one, this divinization and fundamentalizing of mediating instruments is more usually related to the way you understand the faith. Theories about how, for instance, the death of Christ has availed for your salvation. You've got to hold to a particular theory of that in the evangelical church.

Scripture is clear that Christ's death somehow is responsible for our healing, but it doesn't offer a very explicit theory for it. It offers plenty of metaphors instead. Now, there is a certain kind of mind, and I've nothing against it, that isn't content simply to have the experience of the liberation of Christ; it wants to know exactly how it works. What is the metaphysical engineering pattern? There's the theory of substitution which is a part of the metaphor of atonement, derived from St Paul, which claims that Jesus was put to death instead of us, substituted for us, took our punishment. There are other metaphors used by Paul to define the work of Jesus, but this one seems to be an essential piece of dogma that you have to buy to be an evangelical. If you don't you are thought to be unsound, you're maybe not even saved. So these things become not interesting topics for discussion to help us all along - useful ways of sharing our faith with each other - but ways of including and excluding, back to what we were saying earlier about being in or out.

Brice   But the parables are metaphors and you presumably don't object to the use that's made of them. In any event trying to understand the metaphysical engineering pattern might be a valid way in for some people ...

Richard   Perhaps I'd better explain a bit more about my angle on the use of metaphor in the Bible.

Brice   I'd like that.

Richard   In the New Testament there are a number of ways in which the writers try to explain the effect of Christ on their lives. To do this they use figures of speech; metaphors. In a metaphor we take one thing and apply it to another. The word means 'carry over'. All religious teaching is metaphorical in this sense. We don't get God neat. God is conveyed by language and experience, but there is always a sense in which God comes *through* and is not to be overidentified with the word or the symbolic system that is used. The New Testament uses three main metaphors to describe the liberating effect of knowing Jesus: justification, redemption and sacrifice. In the first metaphor, a legal one, we are guilty but, because of Jesus' work, we are let off, justified, judged innocent. In the second, we are slaves but God pays our ransom price in Jesus and frees us. In the third metaphor, the idea is that Jesus bears our burdens for us, sacrifices or substitutes himself for us, pays our debts. These are all useful ideas, but it is unwise to push them too far. Metaphors work by surprise and suggestion, not by some kind of legal precision.

Brice Which, I suppose, is why you get so vexed by people who try to present metaphors as The Truth.

Richard And it is an interesting fact that the ancient Church, so keen to define so much, did not seek to define the mystery of Christ's saving work. It is almost as though it recognized that this mystery is so deep that we'd never pin it down in any single series of metaphors. It freed us to find others. You, for instance, are already working on an interesting modern metaphor which describes the work of God in Christ as a way in which we are reparented. We'll come to that later.

Brice Of course, with my background, I think that there is a great deal of good stuff in the evangelical way of looking at things, in the evangelical vessel. But there are ways in which we become enslaved by certain metaphors. One thing that bothers me is the way in which the atonement theory, as opposed to the atonement metaphor, with its step-by-step, almost mechanical, progression from the Garden of Eden through sin and the resurrection to heaven, is so appealing to young minds. It was to mine when I became a Christian at the age of twelve, it still is, it helps me to know what I believe. The problem is that to some extent it is also responsible for keeping evangelical Christian minds young. Let me explain. Young evangelical Christians facing the emotional, physical and spiritual complications and questions of adulthood are rather left to wallow and fend for themselves by many evangelical leaders. This kind of leader tends to be rather legalistic and black-and-white in their approach to questions of Biblical interpretation and dogma. I'm thinking of things like forgiveness, sin, sexuality, guidance, salvation and so forth. Maybe in an attempt to keep things manageable and explainable we get . . .

Richard   A bit fundamentalist at times . . .

Brice   Partly that, but partly also that in an attempt to keep things manageable and explainable the whole picture of life is not presented as explorable to the young of this particular vessel. The church lets them down by not giving them a bigger human view so - and you might be expecting this by now - they do one of three things when they become adults. Firstly they might stay childish - not childlike - in their spirituality and sometimes even become fatuous. Secondly, they might repress and deny the infantilizing aspects of the institution and so find a way of rising above it. They become more spiritually mature than the vessel they ride in.

Richard   And thirdly, they have a habit of jumping onto the overcrowded number forty-two municipal omnibus and never coming back.

Brice   Er, precisely, Bishop.

Richard   Fascinating how the vanities of the various church traditions have so much in common as we dig into them. You faithfully describe the shortcomings of the church tradition that you belong to, but it is true in different ways of all the churches I know too. This, I suppose, means that we are all wonderfully human.

Brice   There's a bit more I want to say on the evangelicals which might be true of other denominations as well. My observation is that the childish and fatuous church members that I described a minute ago are often the ones who look for positions of power.

Richard   This is definitely true of other denominations as well . . .

Brice   Perhaps that's where they feel safe.

Richard   Such people often get the power they want because they are seen to be people who actively represent the culture.

Brice   The problem is that they then let the young people down in exactly the same way they were let down and so it goes on.

Richard   What does that do to a church?

Brice   What I think it does to the evangelical church is to create a culture of answers. Questions of certain kinds are not encouraged. They are too threatening to the culture so the culture tries to make them irrelevant. And it doesn't just do it with ideas, it does it to the people attached to them as well. For instance, I had been a Christian for several years before I found out that I am part of a particular tradition, the evangelical tradition. I just thought I was a Christian and that was it. I didn't until much later ask questions of other traditions, I just dismissed them or worse, I ignored their existence and the people who live in them.

Richard   This brings us neatly to our next topic.

Distorting the Authentic Voice of Jesus

Richard   One of the most encouraging aspects of the New Testament is the way the disciples of Jesus constantly got it wrong. There is a lot of stuff in the Bible about perfection, but the actual human record doesn't show much of it.

Brice   Why do you find that encouraging?

Richard   Mainly because I'm imperfect and would feel uncomfortable in a perfect community. But there is a more serious point to be made.

Brice   Make it then.

Richard   How do you get to be good at, say, tennis? Do you start out good?

Brice   Practice, I guess. Playing the game a lot.

Richard   Precisely, and the same is true of life and it's true of Christianity. There is a developmental side to it. It takes practice. But there is this weird notion that religious people, especially *real* Christians, should already be perfect. That's a bit like expecting someone to be a 'good' tennis player who's had hardly any practice. It takes a lifetime to be good in the Christian sense, so telling someone to 'be good' is a waste of breath.

Brice   It doesn't stop people getting up in the pulpit and doing just that. They miss the point and cripple people with guilt.

Richard   They do, but the Christian faith is a way of helping imperfect human beings develop, become good, if you like.

Brice   And you think the Church sometimes distorts that message?

Richard   Oh, it constantly does that. For instance, let's take power as an example. One part of the tradition that speaks most obviously with the authentic voice of Jesus is the opposition to abuses of power. The fact that his own apostles got into these struggles – power struggles, if you like, – broke Jesus' heart. He was constantly trying to get them to leave all that behind. This is well illustrated in Mark chapter ten when the sons of Zebedee want a special place in his kingdom – the kingdom of heaven – and the other apostles hear and they think, 'Damn it, they've beaten us to it. They are going to be made Chancellor and Home Secretary'.

Brice   It had started even then.

Richard   It had started even then and they were completely uncomprehending. But Jesus tells them that his outfit was not going to operate that way, it was not to be like that among them.

Brice   But it does operate like that.

Richard   It operates exactly like that. Now okay, soon the

Church had huge numbers in its congregation, people to feed, widows to look after, and missionaries to support and send out. It had to get organized and in some ways the institutions that developed have worked and worked quite well. The real problem comes when instead of just being an administrative structure the organization of the church gets sacralized and made part of the message of Jesus that it never was originally.

Brice We seem to have a need to justify and aggrandize our spiritual activities. In the process of sanctifying them we make it countercultural to contradict or question them: it can become heretical to question the institution or to want to do things differently. Sometimes it even becomes heretical to experience God differently from the norm set by the group. In an effort to preserve the integrity of the memory and message of Jesus, and to follow the prompting of his Spirit, we create separate internally noncontradictable cultures. Of course, at the heart of all the various bits of sanctified human vanity are often important and authoritative parts of Jesus' message and memory - it's how they start. This means that if someone questions the vanity they run the risk of being rebutted as if they are attacking the spiritual reality that often lies, albeit rather hidden, at the centre.

Richard Frustrating.

Brice I think it is often impossible for someone to join a Christian institution - a church - without consciously, or unconsciously, burying part of their humanity - themselves - to try to get comfortable with the quite shameful and outrageous distortions of Jesus' message that can go on. No wonder so many people find themselves experiencing a loss of their faith when they try to grow as people, when they try to find out more about their personhood.

Richard   Can you give me a couple of examples of the way in which our personhood, as you put it, can be hurt by church institutions?

Brice   Well, I can tell you a story and see what you make of it.

Richard   Fine.

Brice   A friend of mine fell in love with a girl recently and he is the sort with a tendency to discover his passions in difficult circumstances. The girl is a Catholic and lives in the US; he is Episcopalian and lives in Britain. Well, when he is Stateside he goes to church with her and the priest gets up and says: 'Now we're going to pray for everyone in purgatory. Purgatory is the place where you receive the punishment due for sins forgiven'. My friend thinks to himself 'If my sins are forgiven then why do I need punishing for them?' And all these people around him are supposedly praying for their dead aunties, or something, so that they won't have too rotten a time of it in purgatory – something that was invented in the third century AD – and it doesn't mean anything to him; as far as he's concerned he prays for forgiveness and that's it. Anyway they talk and spend time with each other and try to pray together, you know, out loud, which is normal for him when with others and of course he prays directly to Jesus and she explains that it is normal for her to pray to Mary and the saints to intercede with Jesus. They talk a bit more and the subject gets onto being sure that you are a Christian and going to heaven and he explains that once he has committed himself to following Jesus then that's it, he's joined the elect and he's on the roll, so to speak. She explains that for her nothing is certain and it depends on how faithful she is to the Church.

Richard   They split up?

Brice They split up. Now there may have been all sorts of reasons why they split up but one was certainly that my friend thought that they were worshipping different gods. I don't think that was the case, in fact I think that what got between them was their respective experiences of the institutionalization of the memory of Jesus. Now, I don't know much about Catholicism but in the churches I do have experience of, house churches, Anglican churches, and the like, I've come across uncertainty and guilt being used to manipulate people. Is the same thing happening here?

Richard How do you mean?

Brice Well, for instance, of purgatory, I wonder why a system has developed that seems to put divine forgiveness, and by implication divine acceptance, on the end of a string - just out of reach. And with all the rules and dogma surrounding assurance of salvation - whether you're really going to heaven or not - I wonder why a system has grown up that seems to use uncertainty as a central tenet? You see, if I wanted to create an institution, religious or otherwise, that controlled people *en masse* I would put a premium on uncertainty and guilt; people would never feel safe to leave the building. I'd have them by the ears.

Richard I don't think you quite understand Catholicism here. Unsurprising in someone brought up in the evangelical tradition. It's difficult to enter another religion's mindset, but worth trying, even if you prefer your own for most purposes . . .

Brice I've got a feeling you're about to expose me to the Catholic mind.

Richard You bet. And the first thing to recognize about

Catholicism is that it is baptized paganism. Another way of putting it is to say that it sought, not to deny nature, but to perfect it. When Pope Gregory sent Augustine to England he was told not to destroy the pagan customs of the English but to baptize them, take them over and sanctify them for Christ. That is why many old churches are built on ancient pagan sites and it is why many of the Church's festivals are Christianized versions of old pagan feasts, such as Christmas, which is a Christian version of the winter solstice celebrations. The principle behind this is important. It suggests that our natural struggle to understand and worship God is not to be despised, it is to be fulfilled. The Christian faith fulfils, it does not deny, our natural religion or our natural reason. That is why there is something called the development of doctrine in the Catholic, particularly the Roman Catholic, tradition. Take the doctrine of purgatory that got your friend into trouble. It is based on a fairly straightforward, in fact, rather compassionate principle. Most of us are imperfect but God is burning holiness. Most of us live in some kind of darkness, but God is light unapproachable. If we were to die today it stands to reason that we could not immediately bear the holiness and blinding glory of God's presence. So, it is suggested, there will be a time after death in which to get cleaned up and used to the light, a kind of preparation.

Brice   And that's what purgatory is?

Richard   Well not exactly, but it's the idea on which purgatory is based. There is a logic to it. Unfortunately, human beings have a tendency to elaborate simple ideas into complex structures and that's what happened here.

Brice   And it's what my chum fell foul of.

Richard The Latin Church with its genius for system and elaboration went overboard on answering unanswerable questions. That was a kind of intellectual excess and it led to the kind of moral excesses that helped precipitate the Reformation, when the papacy tried to raise money by auctioning indulgences, a way of buying your dead relatives remission from purgatory.

Brice But don't you think the idea is intrinsically corrupt?

Richard No, but there is a tendency in religion to claim too much, especially about the afterlife. I think it is best to leave all that to God's loving purposes for us.

Brice Your explanation is clear and helpful. My story illustrates how confusions can occur and become a powerful basis for division and even mistrust between the various traditions. Nevertheless, for many people, albeit usually those disaffected with the Church, there is a strong sense of manipulation and coercion within the Church. Thinking of the other end of the spectrum, I have observed the house churches using uncertainty and guilt to manipulate their congregations. One of the things that these sort of church groups tend to do is put a premium on levels of spirituality and it goes in this sort of order: whether or not you are really saved; if you are, have you been baptized in the Spirit; and, if you have been, which of the gifts do you manifest? If you manage all that, in some of these setups, the question is: are you sound enough to be an apostle? Uncertainty and preoccupation about levels of personal sanctity, as well as guilt about unconfessed sin, are often the results. Now it might all be based initially on simple New Testament stuff but it soon becomes a way of the institution keeping people in line.

Richard   Right, I'm with you so far, but where does this get us?

Brice   There are three responses to the above which we would expect to see if there is any accuracy in my observations. They are the ones I mentioned before. Some people would be in church all the time, others would find a way of denying and repressing the sense of guilt and uncertainty so they can have some sort of faithful life within the institution and others would say, 'Stuff it, I'm not buying into this any more!' and leave.

Richard   Okay, the first one is familiar, the last one is as well, if you laid end to end all the angry, guilt-ridden lapsed Catholics . . .

Brice   And bruised and embittered people who have tried to escape from the house church movement to name but two . . .

Richard   But you'll have to go a bit further with the second one; can you, he said, knowing the answer, give me an illustration?

Brice   Sure, consider this; people come out of church smiling and chatting. They don't, usually, come out panic-stricken and looking frantically for help or jump straight on to the number forty-two vowing never to come back. Some do, and they are often the most clear-headed, but the majority of us come out smiling and chatting. To do this we either have to have repressed the guilt and uncertainty of the institution or have found a way of rising above it. If it is repression, I wonder what else we have repressed with it - more of that in the next chapter - and if it is that we have risen above it then surely we are more spiritually mature than the institution we are a part of and I wonder that we can stand it.

Richard   My observation and, if you like, my hope is that the

Church continues to evolve. All this is part of our evolution.

Brice I'll agree with that, I agree that we are evolving and I think it is also true that the Church is, so to speak, good enough as it is.

Richard The Good Enough Church. I like that.

Brice So do I. The Church does the job okay; it's survived, God makes sure. We must accept that we will never have a perfect Church. However, and it's a big however, the fact that it is good enough in total, and fine for many individuals, doesn't stop it obscuring the liberation of Christ from some, blocking the growth of others, and destroying the lives of still others.

Richard So there is stuff to be faced and there is work to be done. Especially by those already in the churches somewhere who think its going all right thanks.

Brice If they aren't too sleepy, yes.

The Power and the Glory

Just What is Power?

Richard   One of the things that took years to dawn on me was that power is an important issue in churches. I am not referring to so-called 'spiritual power'; the authority that, allegedly, comes from God and is exercised by a human representative of God. That way of putting it itself raises interesting issues that we ought to explore. It can be a disguise for the straightforward exercise of human power. I'm not thinking about that . . .

Brice   What are you thinking about?

Richard   You know how some people seem to be more interested in power than others, more status-conscious, more protective of their rights than others? Well, it comes as a surprise to find so much of that in the Church.

Brice Why particularly?

Richard Because it is so obviously at odds with the example of Christ. He was quite precise about the matter. Mark's gospel in chapter ten describes a power struggle among the apostles and Jesus points out that this was the world's way, 'But it shall not be so among you,' he went on. It is always a bit of a shock when the Church so blatantly contradicts the standard of Jesus. This is where you come in. I suspect that these struggles over who should be in charge of anything and everything, from the flower rota to the government of the Universal Church, tell us a lot more about the individuals concerned than about anything else. The conflicts are clothed in the language of principle, even theology, but there is really something else going on. That's why I think we ought to look at the way human beings handle power.

Brice Fair enough. What's your question?

Richard I want to start by asking you to define power in the human context. Can you do that?

Brice I can try. I think I would describe power as the perceived ability to influence the future of ourselves and others.

Richard That's succinct. I notice that you are implying that there is a difference between actual power and our sensation of power.

Brice It's very important to distinguish between the inner and outer worlds of the individual where power is concerned. For example, it is perfectly possible for someone to consider themselves as possessing little real power but in fact for them to be very influential in the lives of others. Equally, it is possible for someone to consider themselves to be powerful and to be blind to, or surprised by, the apparent lack of response from the world around them.

Richard Sounds familiar. What might be going on in the internal world of someone who needs to be powerful like this? If I've used the expression correctly.

Brice You have, and it is not an easy one to answer. The first thing to consider is that if we are like this person, and most of us are at times, then deep down we probably feel very weak and powerless. A great many things may have led to a sense of weakness, powerlessness or irrelevance in us and some of it may be manageable from day to day. If it is not - because the fear and vulnerability that it generates is just too much - we may be forced to mount an unconscious defence to it; push it down, deny it exists. We don't want to be overwhelmed by it or, to be more accurate, overwhelmed by the fear of being overwhelmed by it. We need our defences until we feel safe enough to realize how they limit us. For instance, someone listening to what I've just said might be convinced that it doesn't apply to them. It might not, but if it does it has to be denied for the present. They don't feel safe enough yet.

Richard Digressing for a minute. What makes *you* feel safe enough to come out from behind *your* defences?

Brice Two things. The knowledge that I am known as I am and accepted as I am by you, for instance, and by God.

Richard Easy?

Brice No, terrifying. And I'm not very good at it.

Richard The other thing?

Brice Frustration. The same frustration that a butterfly must feel when trying to push its way out of a hard and unyielding chrysalis. The chrysalis that has protected it while it is vulnerable has now become a suffocating prison.

Richard It's a help to know that you shrinks are like the rest of us. Getting back to the subject, tell me what other defences there are against inner powerlessness.

Brice Often it is a thing called reaction formation which we've mentioned before in chapter one. Reaction formation is the adoption of behaviour opposite to that which would reflect our true feelings and impulses. This process is, of course, unconscious and so goes on without us realizing. I might infer you are doing it from what I observe. If, deep down, you felt powerless and inferior and were not able to bear this knowledge then you might go to great lengths to appear powerful and superior to others.

Richard I would be doing this to be in control.

Brice Exactly. What is crucial here is to see how the inner world of the person and the outer world around him, the world of others if you like, are influencing one another. This applies to us all, because we all do it, even if only a bit. In his inner world someone in this situation will have created a way of coping with his unacceptable feelings which will require acting upon in the outer world for their validation. The flaw in all defences, and it gives them away every time, is that they won't stand up on their own. We need others to join in our defensive dramas otherwise they will come crashing down. This is usually a thing too terrible to contemplate without help. If it could be contemplated then the defence would not be needed and it would soon evaporate.

Richard But if it can't, then, as we've seen before, other people will respond in characteristic ways to someone being superior and controlling all over the place. I expect they might withdraw from him, despise him or find ways of getting around his attempts to control so that eventually his worst fears will end up realized. Will he become more and more desperate? What will happen then I wonder?

Brice He might leave the church, get depressed or have some sort of crisis that may help him to come to terms with the way he really feels about himself. If the person in this example is the minister then the people around him might leave or simply withdraw their energy and commitment instead. You see, the only time that the inner world of the individual and the outer world of everyone else can really come into contact is when there are very few defences on either side. That's the real starting point; we never move on from some unwelcome feeling about ourselves, whether it contains truth or not, until we can bear to contemplate it. If only for a little at a time, and for that we need each other. You began by asking me what power is and I hope I have left the impression that the inner sensation of power is one that is open to great counterfeit and confusion and, as a result, can be the basis of much unholy activity. The outer-world aspects of power are all at the mercy of the perception, interpretation, and action of the individual, who is acting on what is in his own inner world.

Richard Quite a tangle.

Brice Quite a tangle, and yet, I think it is worth struggling to find out more about how power is given, received, brokered, and misused amongst Christians. If we succeed we will be better equipped to discriminate clearly between the toxic and nourishing aspects of power in church life.

Richard We are talking about human nature in one of its most problematic and interesting aspects. I want to keep everything you've said so far in mind and broaden out our discussion to what you've called the 'outer-world' aspects of power. I can't help feeling that the way in which the inner world and outer world interact touches at the very essence of what it is to be human. To grow and develop towards our full potential we need a healthy way to handle all this stuff and it needs to be a way that is conducive to human flourishing. This would apply not only to the church but also to the office and the family. In most ways the church is no different, it is simply another place in which these dramas are worked out. Maybe there's sometimes less honesty in the way the church handles them. We are not really supposed to be engaged in power games so we pretend we aren't. What's the healthy way ahead, Doc?

Brice We need to be more honest about what might be going on, perhaps in ourselves, that underlies any power-related activity we might get caught up in. I am thinking of those things which are usually pushed from view like our motivations and our ulterior motives.

Richard I can see that it might be salutary to stop and reflect but how will it actually help? It sounds hard and potentially painful. Surely we are always going to have some ulterior motives for everything we do? Aren't you just lumbering us all with a sort of counsel of perfection?

Brice No, that's not the idea. It would, however, be a misunderstanding that someone might find hard to shake off if they wanted to dismiss what I am going to say next.

Richard   Which is?

Brice   Simply that the point behind what I *am* saying is to help us find choices where we previously thought none existed. If I'm trying to lumber us with anything it is with more choice.

Richard   But surely power gives people choice.

Brice   That all depends upon whether or not it is being handled in a toxic or nourishing manner. When there is power around, and I mean simple practical things like who is in charge or who controls the money, then there is plenty of opportunity for individual and group choices to diminish. We get focused on the power and not the job in hand. Power is a very primitive thing; it often feels like, and sometimes is, the difference between life and death. When power is around there is a tremendous urge to behave like our primitive selves.

Richard   Grabbing, snatching, scheming, that sort of thing?

Brice   Just that sort of thing. After all why do you think people say they feel a sense of relief when they have got rid of some responsibility or other?

Richard   They are no longer a target?

Brice   Correct answer. Your turn.

Richard   Same question again. What's the healthy way ahead?

Brice   A good place to start is to realize that if we want power, want influence, want to be the leader then, in a sense, we would be better off waiting. We are, moreover, likely to be lacking in the personal maturity necessary to be nourishing with it. Reflect, for a moment, on what so often happens when people who strive for power over others, get it. Power doesn't corrupt, power in the hands of those who can't handle it corrupts.

Richard Speculating, I wonder if many of us are driven, compelled from within, to seek more power than we can handle.

Brice That's one side of the coin and the other is that some others push away what they could handle if they tried. Neither person is finding out what it is to be themselves. They are both being something they are not and when we do that we are showing that we believe, at a deep level, that we have no choice. This is not the case. It is all part of the strange human compulsion to keep doing the things that destroy us from inside.

Richard We are going to talk more about that later when we think about sin.

Brice Indeed so. I'll get back to your question. The healthy kind of power is the kind that people have proportionate to their own inner security and sensitivity to themselves and others. If I can live with myself the way I really am – I don't have to like all of it – then I will be more complete, more integrated, if you like. Someone who is reasonably well integrated and at home with their own inner spontaneity is naturally powerful. People will want to know what they have to say, people will follow them. One way in which we can think of Jesus is as fully integrated both humanly and spiritually. He didn't need or search for power, he was fully integrated, he had it because he didn't need it. When the two are balanced like that it is tremendous. It's natural. It is about being a powerful person.

Richard Thinking about that, I'm struck by how much traffic there is across the bridge between the inner and outer worlds.

Brice Indeed. The more the reality of the inner world resembles the reality of the outer world the less necessary it becomes for our unconscious to alter things as they cross to and fro over the bridge.

Richard We need help with this sort of thing, and yet I see many people in power putting themselves beyond help, refusing to acknowledge that they need it.

Brice Being available for help also means being vulnerable so it is easy to see why this is the case. We learn to despise vulnerability. Very often the hidden motivation behind getting power is to escape feelings of vulnerability. It is a common observation in my game that if someone is using their power to be cruel to others they are, unconsciously, seeking relief from the abiding memory of cruelty done to them when they were powerless.

Richard Such as when they were children?

Brice That's when we are at our most vulnerable to cruelty and also the time where the seeds of our own cruelty are sown.

Richard How so?

Brice It's what we call 'identification with the aggressor'. It is the process by which the child, sensing that the person being cruel to them is, in practical terms, less vulnerable than they are, learns to link security, power and cruelty together. As children like this grow up they seek power over others through cruelty. Using cruelty they will achieve a sense of relief from their own, quite unbearable, feelings of vulnerability and insecurity. The most available and defenceless victims for our cruelty are our own children, but anyone who can't or won't get away from us will do. Unless we can own up to what is happening and choose to do it differently then the whole thing gets passed on to the next generation. After all, who has ever met a bully who has not himself first been bullied?

Richard This is what that sad old man the poet Larkin meant when he wrote:

Man hands on misery to man,
It deepens like the coastal shelf.
Get out as quickly as you can
And don't have any kids yourself.

Brice Before we move on I should make clear that many of the stories I tell of how we can be toxic to ourselves and others are a perversion of things that are more naturally nourishing. For instance, think how different the story is when the child's vulnerability is responded to by the powerful person they are relying on with kindness, gentleness and acceptance. In a way I am describing an experience that we yearn for from God, and which he offers.

Richard I'm surprised. I was going to ask you if things like our cruelty can be put right even when we are adults and I was expecting you to bung in an advert for psychotherapy . . .

Brice Instead of revving up to talk about the healing power of the Holy Spirit or miracles or something? Let's save that for later.

Richard Okay, but let me pick up on what you alluded to there. I notice all sorts of parallels between your business and mine, between being a shrink and being a minister, and you've put your finger on an important convergence here. You are suggesting that many of our adult problems are caused by early rejection, early abuse. We abuse because we are first abused, we bully because we are first bullied. This language is a reverse echo of Scripture. John tells us, 'We love because we are first loved.' Our ability to love is a gift, an original endowment by our parents. And the opposite. In the spiritual life it is important to discover that we are first loved by God as we are, with all that we know against ourselves. Alas, much religion starts at the other end. It begins with a god who seems to be permanently angry with us. The reason we call the Christian message good news is because it announces that we are first loved. Knowledge of that love can give us enormous security and makes it possible for us to be honest about ourselves. Back to why we seek power.

Why Do We Seek Power?

Richard Well why do we?

Brice Power which is sought in an unconscious attempt to diminish inner vulnerability is the sort of power likely to be toxic to others. The defensive kind. If we need power in large quantities it may betray a hidden need to counteract unbearable feelings of low self-esteem. If this is our predominant motivation for, say, seeking election to a committee then there is an opportunity for toxic repercussions. We are, here, firmly in the world of the unconscious defence against things we don't want to know about. The things we can't afford to know about.

Richard You'll have to expand on that a bit.

Brice We are denying and repressing the way we really feel, who we really are. It gets toxic for others when we force them to become part of our bogus drama, a party to our self-deception. If we are in a position of leadership, this effect can be particularly powerful but always ends in a kind of aching stagnation. The only way we can mature is to face our self-deception. Until we can, we are living a lie and we are stuck. So is anyone else who is taking part in the drama with us. In the family situation we have an interesting twist to the plot: if you have children you are instantly powerful. You have power given to you when that power may be beyond your maturity to cope with it. As we know, some people actively seek a powerful position and others have it foisted upon them.

Richard I suppose there must be a bit of both in many church leaders, whether they are clergy or laity.

Brice In variable amounts, yes. The moment someone becomes a minister they are given power. They suddenly have a family, and it may be a huge one. Now, and this might seem a big jump, it is an everyday observation that many people have children before they are even able to look after themselves. It is not by chance that these same people have often had pretty miserable childhoods themselves and have a strong unconscious desire for a relationship based on dependency.

Richard Why dependency? I would have thought that if someone has had a rotten time at the hands of their parents they would want to be independent as soon as possible. They would avoid getting close enough to anyone to risk getting hurt again.

Brice That's a reasonable assumption, but this is where we hit an interesting paradox of the human condition. A person has to be very badly hurt in order to despair of ever finding good relationships in the future. If they have been cruelly treated or emotionally deprived to a more usual extent they tend to be desperate for good relationships. So much so that someone like this will tend to squeeze others to try and make them be what they need.

Richard Why?

Brice Hope. The hope that it can be got right at last. The hope that out there somewhere is the good mother or good father that they never had. The catch is that by this time the looked-for 'good person' has become idealized into perfection.

Richard And what more perfect thing than a baby?

Brice Having a child is a good way of sidestepping much of the uncertainty of making relationships with someone who already exists, such as another grown-up. The other important aspect to this is that babies and children are almost completely dependent on those who care for them: the care-giver is in complete control. The unconscious hope in the care-giver is that this time it is going to be different. They are, in a sense, preparing to re-enact their own childhood through the baby and make a better job of it. Sadly this is unlikely to work.

Richard Why?

Brice Because they are not able to see the baby clearly for what it is - another person. Instead, the baby is being used as a mirror to reflect back to the parent bits of themselves that weren't carefully enough looked after when it really mattered. The baby is an unwitting player in a defensive drama mounted by the parent to try and find comfort and meaning for themselves. All parents are like this to some extent and all relationships have a little of this in them. Usually the baby manages to learn its lines well enough to satisfy the needs of the parent whilst, at the same time, it works out how to get some of its own needs met. This is where we learn what life is about and what defences we need to make it bearable. The problem is that our defences, which helped us survive and manage our needy parents when we were children, become a terrible drag when we are older. Put simply, it is very difficult for us not to keep mistaking the outer world and the people in it for players in a continuous re-enactment of our early life. My observation is that this is particularly so in the emotional hothouse of the church.

Richard You're slipping the lid off a huge can of worms here. Tell me what happens to the mirror-baby.

Brice Things start off fine but, if the needs of the parent are too great, the baby simply won't be able to act well enough in the drama to satisfy its mum or dad. To make things worse the baby's own needy demands become more and more strident. The baby will sound to the parent just the same as the parent sounds to herself deep down inside. Isolated, desperate and useless. In extreme cases the emotional abuse will turn into physical attack because the baby makes the parent feel worse, not better. The baby has seemingly done the exact opposite of what it was created to do. Everything it does points at the parent's own inner pain, constantly rubbing salt in the wounds. The baby will be rejected and, if it is lucky, get taken into care before it's too battered.

Richard I've guessed why you are telling me all this. It wasn't hard. I've known churches so battered and deprived that they have had to be taken into care. What goes so wrong?

Brice Before I try to answer that, I want to pick up on something I've just said and develop it a little. I said that one of the tendencies for some people when they don't get what they need as infants and children is to seek for a perfect replacement later on. One possibility is a newborn baby and I'll work on that in a minute but the other is, of course . . .

Richard   God.

Brice   As you say, God. For many people this, and evidence like it, shows that we have invented God out of our own neurotic need.

Richard   And that's not what you believe?

Brice   No. For me, it means that our understanding of the human psyche is reasonably on course. Psychodynamics points a finger that we can follow towards God. For me it helps validate his existence. Anyway, back to the parallel of the parent and child; it is going to be useful to us.

Richard   Are you suggesting that instead of having babies, or as well as, some people, predominantly men, have churches in order to try to fill a gap in their inner world? That it is a way of seeking out dependent relationships? They need to be needed?

Brice   Yes, and we can see very clearly the similarities between what I have outlined above and what so often happens to those in prominence in the church. These people sometimes become what I call 'chronic givers'. Having given up hope of finding a spontaneous sense of meaning in themselves, they look to others to provide it for them. They look after others in the unconscious hope that the resulting gratitude and admiration will at last give them the inner meaning they crave. Moreover, for Christians, there is the hope that this sacrifice will be enough to make God really love us. God's love is hard to accept as a free gift so we try to earn it. I know this sounds a bit tough on well-meaning types, but it has to be faced. Besides, I count myself in this group. I call it 'taking disguised as giving' and I've seen it in many people in my profession. I've known it in myself, and I've seen it as a large and unrecognized motivation in many Christian workers.

Richard I will let you get away with that because I've seen it often enough, but I want to enter a caution here. There seems to be a category of humans so special as to defy the normal pathologies that characterize the rest of us. For want of a better word we can call them saints. They are people who possess a healthy capacity for total self-giving. I've known one or two. They care for others without neurosis, without any apparent feeding of their own neediness. They have an interesting effect on those who like to control others. Saints break the rules because they are intent only on the other. They respect no boundaries, are not bound by the process and proper rules of engagement. Like other kinds of genius they have to be left to get on with it, but there are obsessive managerial types who cannot cope with this threat to their tidy universe and they baffle the saints who can't understand what all this fuss over regulations is about. As I say, I've known one or two people like that and you have to let them do things their way, set them free. But they are the despair of all people who put process before purpose. They are the exceptions, however. Most of us have very mixed motives. In T.S. Eliot's phrase, doing the right thing for the wrong reason. But that's all right isn't it? God uses what he can in us.

Brice Of course, but if someone's decision to become a leader in the church is too motivated by this inner world need to mount

a defence against feeling unlovable, then it makes them
potential power-abusers and susceptible to abuse by others.
Where this is going on we can expect certain things to be
observable. Firstly a person in this predicament will be very bad
at setting limits on how much they do because no amount of
positive feedback from the world is ever quite enough. Secondly
there will be personal boundary problems.

Richard You mean, that our private and working lives will
become too mixed up together. We won't have boundaries
around things.

Brice Exactly . . .

Richard I've known that one. Is there a third thing?

Brice Yes. Someone in this position will become exhausted and
increasingly ineffective, but will feel unable to do anything
about it.

Richard This really hits me. I'll tell you about a time in the
middle part of my career. When my children were probably at
their most vulnerable, we always had people living with us.
There was a time when we had a sort of community; we felt that
it was what Christians did. There were curates, students and
often a disproportionate number of people with profound
psychiatric problems. The evening meal was always a
community thing, so there would be me, my wife, my children
and all these other people, some of them were from the local
mental hospital, in various stages of off-the-wallness.

Brice And all the time there were your children wanting more
of you to themselves.

Richard Goodness knows what I thought I was doing. There was, I remember, a kind of self-consciousness in me, almost a sense of, 'This is what a Super Self-Sacrificing Christian does'. I can remember the moment when, in a sense, the light switch went on. I realized I was doing violence to myself and the family in the process of trying to make myself into something. I had bought into the idea that if I couldn't be a terrific Christian monk, then I could, at least, have a kind of monastic extended family and have all these people living with me. Community was what one did. It was the ultimate Christian thing. This was an official religious community, with vows and a rule of life: we had a code of discipline and all that. Anyway, the light came on and clearly the community wasn't working. Now, a sort of symbol of the community was an enormous wooden top made to screw to the kitchen table so that we could all sit round it. Within five minutes of deciding to wind up the community I had a screwdriver out and the top off that table. I wanted that great board out of the kitchen as soon as possible. We were something approaching a nuclear family again. I learnt from that experience.

Brice Was it a relief to face the truth?

Richard In some ways it was quite a relief and in others it was very humbling. I learnt, 'You, Holloway, are not cut out for this kind of thing. Partly because you need a bit of peace and quiet and some control of your life and partly because you were just playing at something you aren't anyway'. I was able, after it was all over, to admit that I am not really all that sociable and that I do need my space and my private time. I was forced to admit that I wasn't a Super Guru with a colossal extended family, when I saw that the kids were paying the price for my vanity. Unfortunately, we only get one life to learn all these difficult lessons. I could do it wonderfully next time round. I was trying to be something I am not in order to get what I needed. Just like the mother with the baby you were talking about, I had created a situation which, I hoped, would feed me and which, in fact, did the exact opposite, just like the parent with the baby. Now, you've talked a bit about how things start to come apart at the seams for church leaders who get trapped in this way. Can you analyse it a bit more?

Brice As you have suggested, by the time someone has got into this awful predicament, there is no easy way out. The church environment is often one that is, ironically, intolerant of human failings. Especially in its leaders. When someone gets to the point where they are forced to consider some sort of adjustment they may not be able to do so. Powerful hidden forces deny them room for personal manœuvre.

Richard Like the people they lead needing them to be powerful, all-giving, superhuman . . .

Brice Yes, that's part of the trap and the rest is in two parts. Firstly, a topsy-turvy moral stricture that has crept into Christianity, which makes it somehow un-christian not to be able to manage. Secondly, the defensive drama that I have been describing is built on an all-or-nothing principle. It is, if you like, very black-and-white; things, people and relationships feel either perfect or they feel like rubbish. Primitive infantile functioning results from this way of thinking and we perceive ourselves as never being quite good enough. We hunt perfection whilst haunted by inadequacy. Our fear that any conscious attempt at readjustment of this toxic situation will result in a sort of catastrophic personal meltdown, or invite attack or humiliation, further maintains our stuck position.

Richard I know what you are going to say next because it is what you always say. Something like 'But, of course, the unconscious is a very powerful thing and it will attempt to make adjustments. Whether we like it or not'.

Brice Correct, and we won't like it because unconscious adjustments, in this sort of very trapped situation, usually make the individual even more trapped and isolated from help (good relationships) and nearly always disadvantage those he is trying to serve.

Richard For example?

Brice Well, the adjustments will have elements of the family breakdown I described earlier. There will also be elements of the behaviour of children who are having problems, but aren't being listened to properly.

Richard Which are?

Brice There are four usual ways: not eating, feeling ill, behaving badly and underachieving at school. In the adult the more dramatic examples of the same thing are depression, addiction, absenteeism and, interestingly, sometimes, a loss of spiritual conviction. As you can see there is a thread running through these things of loneliness, withdrawal from others, self-contempt, and isolation from God. In this case they are the very things that, deep down, we least want to happen. They are the very things that the defence was mounted to avoid. Sooner or later something will have to give. The result will seem out of character to many and it is likely to be bewildering and humiliating for the individual concerned. Thankfully, this story is relatively unusual. What is more common, and, for that reason, more serious, are the less dramatic examples played out over and over again in the church. I am thinking, for instance, of the home-group leader who starts to resent the members of the group, believing them to be demanding and non-contributory. Or the 'Junior Church' leader who can't seem to get enough people to help out and who starts feeding the children too much of her own bewildered view of the world. Then there is the church secretary who was thought to be a real powerhouse but now seems to sigh a lot and make too many mistakes. Another common example is the minister who becomes absent-minded and keeps losing his diary.

Richard   You think that someone will deliberately 'lose' their diary?

Brice   Maybe. Much more likely, their unconscious will save them the bother and lose it for them. Like I keep telling you; powerful thing the unconscious.

Richard   Perhaps it would be easier if the unconscious didn't exist.

Brice   That's what a lot of people think and some deny either its importance or even its very existence. The funny thing is that it is their own unconscious that is mounting this defensive denial against its own objective reality. The unconscious is trying to make itself disappear and thus proving its own existence . . .

Richard   Shut up and drink yer hemlock.

Brice   Fine. There are four points to make about all this. Firstly, we can be reasonably certain that the causal links that I have outlined are reasonable and true because we can predict the outcome of similar situations by using these and similar theories of the unconscious. Secondly, the individuals in the example are partly responsible for the situation they are in.

Thirdly, everyone else is partly responsible for the situation these people are in; and fourthly, these situations are potentially avoidable and remediable.

Richard The first one I can accept – I've got to, otherwise you'll just tell me that I can't face it and I'm denying it.

Brice Old psychiatrist's trick that.

Richard Could you go through the second and third ones together? The responsibility ones.

Brice We have seen how the need for power, influence, recognition and purpose can be part of the motivation for leadership, and no harm in that. It is when it is too big a part that the trouble begins. The home-group leader's anxiety when starting up the group might have made her rather controlling with the result that group members may have buried their own creativity or given it away. They've projected it into the leader. She will be perceived as the one with the answers; the group members will be afraid of saying the wrong thing. Wrong thing? In a Bible study? Surely some mistake. The leader's anxiety will worsen because people aren't contributing or being spontaneous. Of course, the group members are responsible for keeping it going by being passive and demanding. They have learnt their parts in the drama well.

Richard What happens next?

Brice Next, the problems of the overloaded parent manifest themselves with unconscious, but very real, attacks on the group. These will start with seemingly trivial things like no biscuits: 'I thought it was about time someone else got some!', to late starting, sudden cancellations, lack of preparation and, on one occasion I heard of, leaving the group standing out in the cold.

Richard How come?

Brice The leader had forgotten the term had started again after the summer break.

Richard It's that diary again.

Brice Just so. In the second example, the Junior Church leader has got out of her depth but can't afford to admit it. The problem is that because she is sending out waves of 'This is really important to me', and 'I'm really fragile', no one else dares to admit it to her either. Characteristically the way this sort of thing is usually handled is that it is not as an emotional problem but as a practical one.

Richard Which it partly is.

Brice Which it partly is, but, 'Jane is doing a great job and she needs some helpers', replaces 'Jane is struggling personally, how can we help her?' It gets turned into a numbers thing and an impassioned appeal goes out for more leaders. A few people might volunteer but they will be unlikely to stick or, if they do, there will be a lot of bust-ups. Jane's real needs are not being met.

Richard This is familiar. I've come across this in a different context. These sort of appeals seem to put people off rather than encouraging them to join in. It is as if they are sensing something and shying away. Tell me, what does this person really need?

Brice The freedom to stop being a mother to everyone and for someone to be, for a little while, the good daddy she never had.

Preferably not her boyfriend, but that's another story.

Richard   Okay then, what about the sighing secretary?

Brice   Here there is a trade-off between feeling overwhelmed, or unrewarded, and being in control – knowing what is going on. The problem is that if too much of the motivation for becoming the church secretary is a power thing then this person will be unable to say 'no' to things. It will feel too much like failure. This person always has to manage and, because they always do manage, they start to get taken for granted and their sense of their own importance reduces.

Richard   People stop noticing how special the secretary is . . .

Brice   And the sighing starts. It says, 'Notice me, notice me'.

Richard   And nobody does?

Brice   Well they probably won't seem to but, unconsciously, people notice all right and they usually stay emotionally unavailable. After all the reason that the boy kept his finger in the hole in the dike was not simply that he wanted to save the village, he knew if he pulled it out he would get drowned or beaten up by the dispossessed villagers. In this story of the secretary, and it could be anybody, people will be afraid of being drowned by the emotional flood or attacked for seeming to be critical if they intervene.

Richard   So what will happen in the end?

Brice   In these less dramatic examples, a sort of chronic coping will probably grind on with a gradual self-martyrdom followed by shame-ridden resignation, or a massive accusatory and humiliating explosion of feeling. 'Why did no one help me?'

Richard   It all sounds so familiar and tragic and I don't think it needs to happen, does it?

Brice   It depends what you mean by 'needs to happen'. These things are always going on to meet someone's needs, even when it is as costly as it is. There are undoubtedly much better ways of managing our needs for security than like this. Part of the problem is that we are so bad at helping each other.

In the Image of God?

Brice   I want to return to some of the things you said earlier about the difference between divine and human power.

Richard   I think we have tended to tie up power roles in the Church with God himself. The classic image of God is exactly paralleled in the classic image of the Church. It is a pyramid where you have God as the great apex. Victorian theology was quite explicit in this:

> The rich man in his castle,
> The poor man at his gate.
> God made them high or lowly
> And ordered their estate.

There are many authoritarian versions of Christianity and what I think they have done is to take one of the most difficult and potentially toxic things about humanity - our need for hierarchy - and turn it into a virtue. They make it good for its own sake. This is human society trying to mirror in its hierarchical sequence the reality of God. In some ecclesiastical cultures the clergy are even called 'Father' with the dependency relationships being seen as good; obedience is the ultimate Christian virtue. The clergy pledge allegiance to their bishops, bishops to the Pope and so on right up the line. Not only are those in this sort of tradition caught up in a hierarchical confusion, they are also putting a premium on submitting to one particular theology.

Brice If I understand you right, you are saying that this sort of thing leaves us wide open to the potential of a certain form of power-abuse: people's need to belong is used as an instrument with which to rule them.

Richard And the project Jesus seems to have set himself was to challenge all that. Given that God exists at all then he must, in some sense, be the source of all power and all authority. Nevertheless, the New Testament presents us with this paradox: the source of all power limits that power in himself and empties himself of it. That's in the classical language of Philippians. Or to paraphrase Mark chapter ten, 'In the world this is the way they administer things. The strong order the weak, like all rulers, because this is the way they become great leaders. It shall not be so among you: he that would be greatest among you must be your servant because I, the Son of God, the Son of Man, have come among you to serve you'. So we get this extraordinary challenge to power itself from within God, the source of all power, both by the divine example and by Christ's anger at the abuse of power. Sadly, the Church seems to have followed the very patterns of power that Christ repudiated.

Brice You are not, I presume, suggesting that a sort of ecclesiastical anarchy would be preferable?

Richard I don't want to be misunderstood here. Of course, as churches get bigger and more people join then groups have to be formed for certain tasks. Information has to be shared around second and third hand, group norms arrived at and some sort of coordinating chain of command put into effect. This is, if you like, a form of hierarchy.

Brice Sure, but in an ideal world this will be one that nourishes the large church group rather than feeding off it or poisoning it.

Richard There is something so difficult and so human that seems to happen to people, admittedly to some more than others, when they attain positions of influence and power. For most the effects are, I think, minor and they are still very available to God for his use, but for many others the effect is to limit their own and everyone else's spiritual creativity. Can we have a go at exposing this one a bit?

Brice One way would be to look at some very common situations in which those who are in a position of power may, unconsciously for the most part, misuse that power to maintain a position which, we have already seen, is likely to feel insecure.

Richard It's not the position that is insecure, it is the person, and the fear of the vulnerability may be partly what has driven them to seek status. Unconsciously of course.

Brice Right, but just because we do something unconsciously it doesn't mean that we are not responsible for it. Not once it is revealed to us. The examples I have in mind are of the dogmatist, the manipulator and the saboteur. On gaining power the dogmatist will rapidly assimilate, discover, or have brought with him a set of self-serving truths. These will not be presented to those he leads as ideas, opinions, or suggested approaches for living out their faith, but rather as self-evident natural laws -

like the law of gravity - only to be questioned by the weak-minded, or spiritually deviant. These laws are taken to be normative for the group and anyone who doesn't subscribe to them is quickly marginalized. This has the double effect of maintaining the leader's authority and of letting everyone know very clearly how to be a good member of that particular church.

Richard The dogmatist attempts to infantalize people.

Brice That's right, and it can feel very cosy for a while but actually the hidden instruction is 'Thou shalt not explore, here is the breast of Mother Church, suck on that and you'll be fine. Get yourself unplugged and go off exploring, or looking for your own food, and who knows what will happen to you'. This is an abuse of power that in some churches is clearly part of the tradition and stretches back over the centuries. In others, it is easy to find individuals who happily dogmatize over any issue they can think of with the easy illogicality and insensitivity of those who know they have a hot line to God. Often these individuals idealize their own spiritual experience and present it as The Truth to others.

Richard You get this in every tradition, it is very human. Tell me, what about the manipulator, how does he or she work?

Brice Manipulators control other people by keeping them guessing about whether or not they are getting it right for them. They are often people with a good deal of personal charisma and the carrot they dangle is 'Try to work out what you've got to do to please Daddy'. The trouble is, what you've got to do to please Daddy keeps changing. Of course manipulators come in both flavours, male and female so sometimes there is a Mummy to please. Lots of us are suckers for this one

- we want the reflected glory of being in the entourage.

Richard   I remember a celebrated bishop who surrounded himself with an entourage. He seemed unable to operate without it. When he arrived at a function a fleet of cars would pull up together and out would pile this incredible fan-club.

Brice   Tempting stuff . . .

Richard   Don't even think about it. Tell me about the saboteur instead.

Brice   The saboteur is a slightly different creature. On an unconscious level this person wishes to maintain a position of authority which feels precarious or arbitrary. To do this they sabotage attempts by the wider church group to gather information about what is being decided on the group's behalf and how it is being decided. You see, if a church is mature enough to openly monitor and investigate its own operation then it automatically undermines the setting up of what we call arbitrary authority structures.

Richard   Can you give me some examples?

Brice   What I'm thinking of are the secretive groups of two or three people centred around a particular leader. They talk privately and make decisions just by being that bit further ahead of others. The danger is that they may be making decisions, although variously disguised as, 'for the good of the church', which pre-empt those of the legitimate decision-making body and in doing so meet their own needs and serve their own prejudices. I can illustrate this with a story that someone I met at a conference told me about his church. Like many churches this one had a group of elected people - about twelve - who met regularly to make decisions relating to church life on behalf of everyone else. The problem was that there was an unelected arbitrary authority structure working clandestinely within this group. It consisted of the ordained minister of the church and two of the older and longer-serving members of the council. Now it so happened that the various areas of church life were overseen by different members of the council so that the council had, so to speak, a finger in every pie. Now, from time to time, people left the council, others joined and new areas of church life were considered important enough to have a finger in them.

Richard I can see it coming. A word here, a word there, a chance phone call and the gang of three chose someone for each job that came up.

Brice Pretty well, yes. By the time it appeared as an item on the council agenda someone had been approached and privately asked if they wanted the job. The council, by the time this chap joined it, were so well trained that they always just rubber-stamped the decision made by this power-abusing saboteur and his henchmen.

Richard Let me get this straight. They were using their power to circumvent an open and accessible function of the council and hence increase their own power at the expense of the elected body? Why on earth bother? What were they afraid of?

Brice I can only speculate about that. Perhaps the minister felt a bit powerless in open debate and, being unable to trust his council to give him good things, he found ways of taking away their freedom to choose. The strategy used, again unconscious, was to present the council with a *fait accompli* so that creative discussion or objection would feel out of place. The irony is that he would have got better things if he had let his council be more creative. It was not to be.

Richard   I remember a church that I had some contact with a while back where there were a couple of people known as The Management. Every decision had to go through them. This was a very stuck church. Anyway, back to your story. Did your friend have a go at changing things? Was he successful?

Brice   Yes. He carefully pointed out what he thought was going on but in a way that was constructive and not critical or accusatory. He gave plenty of room for people to act positively in response and not just feel trapped or guilty. Things did change, not dramatically, but enough to make a difference. What was interesting, and this helps to illustrate my point, was what was said in response to his pointing out the presence of the arbitrary power structure. One of the henchmen said: 'But the decisions are made in love and prayer, and besides, it avoids embarrassment'. This perfectly demonstrates the 'good motive' justification as well as his own self-serving hidden agenda.

Richard   It was his own embarrassment that he wanted to avoid.

Brice   Yes, open group discussion to select someone from the group for office was hard for him to bear. People would have to say what they thought of each other's abilities. He was an ideal henchman for that particular minister because they had a shared problem: difficulty with open discussion of emotional material. The other comment came from one of the rubber-stampers: 'When you've been on the council longer you will get used to the way we do things'. Unfortunately one of the difficulties with trying to face our defences is that unless we are very gentle with each other, and we must be gentle, there is the risk that confrontation will make us more defensive still, as it did here.

Other People's Power

Richard Okay, let's see where we've got to so far on power. Power is something that has its effects in our inner worlds and in the outer world around us. There is a great deal of traffic between these worlds and the unconscious is often very active in distorting inner and outer realities to try to make them compatible. The unconscious often works hard to push out of sight - to repress - the feelings that we can't bear to face: feelings of powerlessness and vulnerability. You have described ways in which we are drawn to, or create, situations that promote feelings opposite to those which, deep down, we actually have. This is the defence of reaction formation and it only makes things worse in the long run by increasing our feelings of isolation and frustration. A subject that we haven't developed is the role that the rest of us play in the creation and perpetuation of the problems faced by those with power. My belief is that sorting this out is the responsibility of everyone, not just the identified leader . . . I suppose you'd agree with that?

Brice I think so. The issue of how we cope with power that has been invested in others is very important. How we cope depends, more than anything else, on the quality of our own inner world. If a powerful person impinges upon us we will make certain judgments about them which, if carefully examined, could tell us more about ourselves than the person concerned. The response that an individual has to the powerful person will depend on many things.

Richard What things are important?

Brice Important are: the extent to which the powerful individual is believed to have influence over the life of the other, the extent to which the less powerful person feels responsible for giving the other the influence that they have, and, whether or not they are sexually attracted to the powerful person. There is nearly always some projection into the powerful figure. However, the more integrated the person is in their inner world and prepared to let the other person be who they really are, the less this will happen. In this rare but happy state there will be no need for projection unless it simply be in the nourishing form of a little encouragement. This is encouragement based on what they themselves would be capable of in the position of power.

Richard   If it is more than just a bit of encouragement, what then?

Brice   If it is more than just a bit of encouragement it is possible that we are treating the other person as someone they are not. The person doing the encouraging has denied a bit of themselves, split it off and projected it into, or planted it in, the other person. They are now responding to those bits of themself that they don't feel comfortable with but which they are free to see in the other person. The thing is that it can go either way and that is what is responsible for many of the responses to power in the Church that I have come across.

Richard   What do you mean by either way?

Brice   Well, you can project either your creative and nourishing qualities into someone or your destructive or toxic qualities. The most usual good quality is the capacity to be creative and confident which, when they are given away in projective form, lead us into idealization. The other person, the leader, becomes idealized and thus can do no wrong. Everything they do is by definition right, and you, because you have given away that bit of yourself, feel that much more useless.

Richard How so?

Brice Well, idealizing someone is often a flight away from reality. It is an attempt to solve the problem of having mixed feelings: ambivalence about oneself and the person we are idealilzing. The trouble is that it is a false solution; it doesn't work. Indeed, my idealization, say, of you might be an attempt to cloak my feelings of envy, contempt or aggression towards you which in reality often exist mixed up with my healthy admiration of you.

Richard How does idealization differ from admiration?

Brice When you idealize someone you ignore or deny the attributes of that person which don't fit your fantasy about their perfection. Furthermore, idealization leads to dependence on, and subservience to, the idealized person. Whereas the hallmarks of admiration are emulation and imitation.

Richard I know people do idealize church leaders but why should they? After all it limits the idealizer and places a terrible burden on his or her victim.

Brice I'm not sure, but I think it might be a maturity thing. This is a person who is not yet able to contemplate adequately, and tolerate, the existence of good and bad in the same place; either in themselves or others. They cannot tolerate ambivalence inside themselves so they split it in two and give the good bit or the bad bit away to someone else - they project it. So the people around them, who matter, are perceived as either wholly good or wholly bad. That includes themselves.

Richard This is how small children can behave. Why has someone like this not grown beyond this stage?

Brice Probably because they weren't allowed to by their parents or because the parents couldn't cope with the idea of their child discovering that they, the parents, weren't perfect. But of course the child knew inside himself that, say, Daddy was not perfect; and rather than know this consciously, which would have made him feel very guilty and have upset Daddy, he split the knowledge up into two bits. The good bit he gave to his father so he, the father, could go on seeming to be perfect and the bad bit he kept for himself. In this way the child was spared from the guilty knowledge that his father was flawed and they were also spared the terrible depression that goes with knowing that.

Richard So the child unconsciously decides that the only way to preserve its father as omnipotent is to feel awful inside itself. We do that with God sometimes . . . What a thought. Could the child give the bad bit away as well?

Brice Some of it, yes. This is where Mummy cops it: she's not as good as Daddy.

Richard And in a church, what happens there?

Brice One scenario is where there are two leaders, one can do no wrong and the other no right. Of course, I am painting this very black-and-white to get the point over; real life is a mixture of all these extremes.

Richard Familiar toxic stuff especially when it revolves around different theological perspectives or personal styles. But what happens when the idealized leader is discovered, say very publicly, not to be quite so perfect as people believed?

Brice The first thing to say to that is it is amazing how strong the power of denial can be in these situations. 'Everybody's got it wrong . . . It isn't possible . . . You're just jealous . . .' and so on. The second thing is to tell you another little story.

Richard I am comfortable.

Brice It is amazing to look back with hindsight and see that in this particular church, there was so much denial of the less-than-helpful private life of the minister. He was personally charismatic, highly creative and helped a great many people to lead fuller, richer lives as Christians. Nevertheless, he was a time bomb waiting to go off. Eventually the tabloids got hold of it and the clay feet were revealed in a way that could not possibly be denied. What particularly interests us here is that the people's response was in large measure attributable to the degree of idealization they had shown towards this minister. Disillusionment, depression, a sense of betrayal and rage were the reactions of those who had idealized him the most.

Richard Are there any other responses to someone else's power that we should talk about at this point?

Brice Yes, envy. If there was ever a part of our humanity to feel ashamed of it is this. Envy and the deliberate, systematic destruction of others that goes with it.

Richard Those with power come in for a lot of this from time to time. If I have something that someone else wants, why must they run me down, trip me up and deliberately misunderstand me?

Brice Envy makes us destroy the person who has the thing that we want.

Richard I would have thought that if someone has something that we want then the thing to do is set about getting it for ourselves. Leave them to get on with having fun.

Brice But if we want something and don't believe - in the unconscious bit of ourselves - that we are clever, special or important enough to have it, then our negative self-feeling can turn to rage, and our unconscious gets us to believe that it and hence the other person, are both worthless. We do it in order to compensate for the way we really feel.

Richard Once again we behaves the opposite to the way we really feel . . .

Brice And set about destroying the thing we secretly desire.

Richard You are describing a sort of intellectual and emotional vandalism. Clergy are notoriously prone to the sin of envy. Partly, I suppose, it is because there is a career structure in the Church that isn't supposed to be competitive; we are supposed to be in a vocation. We are not meant to indulge in rivalry but we do, and sometimes not very subtly: some people's churches are fuller than others, not everyone can be a bishop, and so on. It is made much worse by the fact that envy, because it is so unacceptable, is denied and pushed underground. Envy is much more destructive that way.

Brice I've nothing to add to that for the moment except to end by pointing out that what we have discussed shows, amongst other things, the paradox of human maturing: our ability is constantly undermined by our insecurity.

Individuals and the
Message of Jesus

The Language We Use

Richard   Let's continue to think about the way individuals in the Church react to the message of Jesus: the message of Jesus to the individual and the individual's response.

Brice   In the last chapter we looked at how the institution impinges on the individual. This time I think we need to discuss how the individual impinges on the institution. This is a tricky area for me: it is much easier to make generalizations about the life of groups than it is to generalize about individuals.

Richard   And tricky for me too, because so much of the language we will be using is metaphorical.

Brice   Explain.

Richard   One of the big difficulties in religious discussion is the status of the language we use. We may use words like Satan or Hell but we can use them in different ways, figuratively or literally. Religious people often don't seem to understand the difference.

Brice   It sounds like you are describing two things there: the way a religious opinion, if stated often enough, can become accepted as a religious fact and the way that words used to describe something spiritual can become holy in themselves.

Richard   Precisely. Some people think that when I say that a religious statement is a metaphor I have somehow undermined it. I haven't. At least, not intentionally. Metaphors are very powerful things. Hell is a very potent metaphor of lostness and disconnectedness. If you tell me that I have to take it literally and believe that there is a place somewhere in the universe where people burn everlastingly, then I would say to you that I can accept that as an image of our wilful rejection of God, but I do not accept it is a geographical fact.

Brice   What about the language of salvation? That must be where much possible confusion lies. I mean when acceptance of a particular metaphor of salvation becomes the basis of salvation.

Richard   An example of that is provided by Bryan Moore's novel *Black Robe*. It's about the Jesuit missions to the Canadian Indians in the eighteenth century. The missionaries went out with a very specific message which a Protestant fundamentalist would understand today. At death we went either to Hell and everlasting torment or to Heaven and everlasting bliss. The only way of getting to Heaven was to give your life self-consciously to Jesus and be baptized in the name of the Father and the Son and the Holy Ghost. No one could be saved except through that formula. They speeded things up by tricking whole villages into saying the words. It was salvation by formula.

Brice I reckon we could save ourselves a lot of confusion if we only remembered that language produces abstract concepts which help us manipulate ideas. There is no magic in the language, it's the truth behind it that counts. What was the result in this case?

Richard Hard to say. In any event it generated a colossal missionary passion and people felt, 'My God, there are millions of souls in this world and they are not baptized and unless they are baptized they are not going to get a chance to live with God eternally'. Anne Dillard provides us with an interesting angle on all of this. More sophisticated missionaries acknowledged that if people had never actually heard the message of Jesus they could hardly be damned for their ignorance. 'If I did not know about God and sin, would I go to Hell?' a hunter asked a local missionary priest. 'No,' said the priest, 'not if you did not know'. 'Then why', asked the Eskimo earnestly, 'did you tell me?'

Brice He's got a point. But I suppose what this illustrates is the ridiculousness of presenting the Gospel in a way that fails to acknowledge and reflect human needs, beyond the central need for salvation.

Richard You find the same approach in some mission societies today and you will find conservative, traditionally-minded Christians who believe the same thing. They confuse the issue for people like me because I believe Christians are called to share their faith, but I also believe that we must examine our motives for doing so.

Brice We have a desire to share what we believe and experience of God. We also have a need for some sort of inner certainty about the future and we have a desire to belong. These are all interrelated in the single concept of fundamentalism.

Fundamentalism

Richard Let me ask you; as a shrink how would you define fundamentalism in generic terms? I'm not now talking in Christian terms because I'm assuming that you will agree with me that it is a basic human phenomenon. It is a very powerful element in the world scene at the moment. There are fundamentalist movements in Islam, in Indian Hinduism, in politics and on social issues like the abortion debate. These are groups of people for whom an issue, whether it is religious, political or ethical, becomes all-consuming and the main focus of their whole life. What's going on when people are doing that? I mean apart altogether from issues of the status of Islam, Hinduism and Christianity as vehicles of the divine – we'll come to that. What do you think fundamentalism is? How do you define it as a human activity?

Brice If we are talking about fundamentalism of the individual, inasmuch as it can be separated from that of the community, then one of the first things that I would say is that people are looking for an improved signal-to-noise ratio. I will need to explain this.

Richard You will.

Brice If a person has a fundamental approach to something then it gives them a pretty unmistakable tune to hum along to: it is a reassuring tune to whistle in the dark. Just as if you tune a radio in to a strong station. There is plenty of signal: the music, and not much noise: the background hiss. On the other hand, if you try to tune in to a very weak station then there will not be much signal but plenty of obscuring noise caused by other competing stations. Life is like that. Full of competing stations. There is far too much stuff coming in for us to stand any real hope of organizing it all. There are just too many decisions, too much to work through.

Richard   And fundamentalism is a way of coping with the overload?

Brice   Yes, coping with the overload is partly the basis of our need to be fundamental; the other part has to do with our need to predict the future, but we'll come on to that. The important thing to realize here is that we all have the capacity to be fundamental and we show it through our prejudices. Our prejudices are like bins we put things in that trouble us but that we can't face. We say we haven't got the time but really it is because we are afraid. I can feel a metaphor coming on.

Richard   It's only to be expected. Carry on.

Brice   Imagine a little village with a tiny post-office. In this village there is a postie who sorts her own mail.

Richard   Okay, I'm imagining . . . It's a happy little village, is that allowed?

Brice   Certainly, for the moment anyway. After all we could do worse than take the view that a child starts off with a predisposition to be whole and happy.

Richard   So this village is a young person and the mail is things coming in that the child's internal postmistress has to sort?

Brice You've been reading the script again, haven't you? The internal postmistress is sorting away and coping well with food, tiredness, tummy upset, Mummy, Daddy, sister, getting cross with doggy, things like that. But of course as the child gets bigger, the world gets more complicated and uncertain. The village becomes a town and the trickle of mail becomes a flood: it is simply not possible to sort it all. Now it is at this point we can see several different responses by the individual to the world around them.

Richard Right, the stuff is flooding in, the world is a complicated place and, if I understand you right, the postmistress has a choice of responses which we need to know about to help us understand fundamentalism. These are unconscious processes: they go on without us realizing.

Brice The first response is to find a way of going on sorting the mail regardless of volume. This is where we can find ourselves *en route* to fundamentalism by easy stages through judgment and prejudice. You see, maybe I simply *have* to stay in control of the outer world, because my inner world cannot cope with the uncertainty and threat of not doing so. This is impossible so I am forced to adopt a method of dealing with whatever comes up in a way that creates the *illusion*, within myself, of being in control.

Richard If you are doing this what happens when you meet a new person?

Brice When I meet a new person I have to have somewhere to put her, if I hear a new idea I have to have somewhere to put that and if I have a new experience I have to have somewhere to put it. This is happening all the time so the sorting bins can't be very numerous; there just isn't time. In terms of the metaphor, the envelopes get sorted into, say, colours and size - nice and neat, nice and tidy - everything under control. The trouble is that a letter to Santa from Susie Short in Sewageworks Lane ends up at the same address as a final demand for the rent to Harry Higginbottom of the High Street.

Richard The North Pole presumably.

Brice As usual, I am painting it rather black-and-white but you can see how prejudice, judgment and ultimately fundamentalism in serving the need for tidiness and control of uncertainty undermine our capacity for creative contact with new ideas, things and people. I don't see an idea, I see something threatening that must be found a bin. I don't meet a new person, I meet someone who is a threat until I can put a label on him. I don't have a new experience: I have the same experience over and over again.

Richard Which is?

Brice Of feeling threatened by anything I don't immediately understand and of having to make it safe by breaking bits off it and smashing it up until it looks like something I do understand.

Richard To make it look like everything else in one of your bins?

Brice Right.

Richard This is interesting. It's making me wonder if it's safe to trust my first impressions of people. Presumably, we all have first impressions?

Brice   Sure, but that is exactly what they are: first impressions. Like the imprint of a printer's plate on a sheet of paper it tells you rather more about the plate than the paper. Incidentally, if someone tells you that their first impressions are invariably right, then beware. What they are telling you is that you have been consigned to a bin, and in that bin you are likely to stay. After all, if you nail somebody into a box it is because you want them dead. That's what coffins are for.

Richard   And what are the other two responses to all these people, ideas and experiences - all this mail to sort?

Brice   One other is, as you might now expect, the number forty-two bus option which in the case of information processing is either madness or suicide. Or both. The third way is the healthy ideal. It depends upon the individual's capacity to tolerate new things.

Richard   As you've said, we can all do these things in differing amounts. I want to know how strong your metaphor is. How does a healthy, well integrated postie cope with the new stuff?

Brice   Well, it might sound a bit odd and fanciful but, in the terms of the metaphor, the postie simply dives into the sea of envelopes and letters and parcels and just swims about. You see, it's not so much about what you do as what you can choose not to do. You can choose not to have to try and make everything safe and at the same time you can choose not to run away from the chaos. I am talking about the capacity to be spontaneous which most of us repress most of the time. We will deal with this much more in 'The Unbearable Feeling of Stuckness'.

Richard This is a good moment for me to pull things together a little. We've talked about how fundamentalism and its cousins prejudice and judgment are caused by an unconscious need to be in control of things that are potentially threatening, like new people, ideas and experiences. What about the other part of fundamentalism that you mentioned; trying to predict the future. Where does that fit in?

Brice This all centres around our need for certainty. *Un*certainty is a fact of life and one that is hard to live with. We have seen the tendency for our inner world to respond by creating the illusion of order where there is in fact chaos. It is a defensive response – defending us against fear of not being in control – and it is a powerful unconscious process: we don't know we are doing it.

Richard But it is an artificial order: big bins and things going to the wrong addresses . . .

Brice It's an artificial order and so, once again, the inner world of the individual and the outer world of everyone else are at odds. Ideas, experiences and people are taken in and often rapidly and spectacularly transformed by the unconscious in a bid to meet the needs of the inner world. The problems really begin when the inner world seeks validation from the outer world by making it act out its own peculiar coping drama or, if you like, its own prejudices, judgments and fundamentalisms. To illustrate this, we could think of a situation in which we suspect fundamentalism occurs, such as the way Christians sometimes deal with morality. We would expect to see many rules and procedures governing the various churches' responses to any event that might occur. They won't be called rules and procedures, but they will be there. One of the hallmarks of a fundamentalist world-view is that it has an answer for everything. It has to have - that's why it exists. In extreme situations the bins are marked with things like 'satanic' or 'unsound'. Things that can't be easily assimilated by the individual are dumped into these. That is not to say that there aren't things that belong in these bins. In many instances, though, they are simply overused.

Richard I've seen groups behaving like this. I'm thinking of churches where this sort of fundamentalist response can become, as you would say, a defence against uncertainty. These people are impossible to talk to and leave me feeling confused and angry. I suppose it is important for them to dump their own unacceptable feelings, like confusion, doubt, greed and lust on to any convenient passer-by. There is something about this need for certainty that underlines the difficulty we find in living with faith.

Brice How's that?

Richard The opposite of faith is not doubt, it is certainty. We don't need faith if we are certain about something. Faith is a kind of trust, something we feel confident about and are prepared to bet on. But it is always characterized by an element of uncertainty. We believe, we trust that God is and that God's nature is love, but we cannot be certain. In Paul's words, we see through a glass darkly. Faith calls for courage and the ability to take things on trust. And something in us hates this kind of uncertainty, so we festoon ourselves with certainties. We claim absolute knowledge about things we can't possibly have absolute facts on. We end up living not by faith but by an increasingly angry series of certainties. Angry, because people challenge them; angry, because maybe deep down inside we doubt our certainties.

Brice When you have a system that has an answer for everything, it gives you the illusion of being able to predict the future. Threats to it are likely to be violently rebuffed. The point of this is to make the present safer to live in. Unfortunately this neat little system is a dead end, it leads nowhere.

Richard Does how we deal with these things depend upon a person's start in life?

Brice Yes. The more generally good and consistent our early experiences were, the more inner security we will start off with. If we were allowed to explore our limitations in an environment of encouragement and acceptance the more likely we are to grow up with enough inner security to live life as an interesting exploration rather than an exercise in trying to make the future less frightening. For most people this ideal formed a part of their early experience, but it is only the starting point. It doesn't have to be the end of the story. The point is that if this was our early experience then we will be more excited by our future than we will be frightened by it.

Richard The interesting thing about all this is that it seems to me to be completely at variance with what I think is the authentic religious impulse. The authentic impulse is about coping securely with an insecure universe in the knowledge that ultimately there is a kind of strength and direction to it. We are accompanied in it, but we are given autonomy and freedom. We are put into scary situations where we have to decide and make up our mind about things. There is not, in fact, a rule book and the noise isn't screened out. It is a very noisy universe. Now, there is a temptation here and it is what philosophers call reifying the divine: making a relative object absolute, a transient fact an eternal one. The Bible calls it idolatry. But this is the temptation that every person, every generation, every Christian community falls for. We cannot settle for the mystery of a God who gives us such an enormous responsibility, who calls us out into a howling wilderness. Instead we want the chosen land, we want the certainty, the security, the golden calves of fundamentalism. The thing that bugs me most as a religious professional, albeit one whom many more convinced believers might doubt the authenticity of, the thing that really gets me about Christian fundamentalists is that they project into me a sense that I am somehow not believing enough. They make me feel that I am not holding on to enough, that my faith isn't of a high enough octane. And, in fact, what I get from them when I am being rational and not threatened is a sense that they in fact are not content to go in faith with the God who is invisible and who yet calls them. They want a God who is positively enshrined in a set of words. They want a positivist understanding of spirituality. This gets them, and us, into all sorts of trouble.

Brice   And yet, like all Christian muddles, there is at the centre a Christian truth. It has become obscured as people have used it according to their own mixed motives.

Richard   This helps me to understand terrible disasters like the Waco tragedy, done in Christ's name. But I suppose you are going to say that the thing that must interest us most here is the smaller and less visible ways in which this goes on in ourselves and so in our churches all the time.

Brice   Yes. Small groups forming around charismatic individuals; uncritical loyalty to a particular explanation of some facet of the Gospel; the creation of splinter churches; an individual turning his or her back on Jesus; these are a few of the common and gently destructive ways in which fundamentalizing can obscure the message of Jesus. It's all an attempt to diminish God and keep us in control.

Richard   But we can't diminish God.

Brice   No, but sinful nature compels us to try. We become less available to God. This should throw up some interesting questions . . .

Richard   Like, how on earth can we be certain that we can trust our response to the person, experiences and ideas of Jesus? How do we ever feel confident enough to share those things with others?

Brice   If we can think like that, we are exhibiting a healthy distrust of metaphor when it comes disguised as The Truth. The little-fundamentalizing that we do to the message of Jesus does just that. By understanding the unconscious processes that compel us to diminish God we might be able to allow Jesus' real message to touch the spontaneity that we all have within us. After all, who needs metaphor disguised as dogma? Who needs prejudiced and fundamentalist responses to the experience of God? Who needs an over-rigid system of explanatory dogma to tame the teachings of Christ? Who needs to control the future for fear that God might move in a mysterious way? Who needs institutions that obscure Christ's message? Who needs to obscure the message of God for others by projecting their own version of it into them?

Richard   You and me?

Brice   Er, well, yes, actually. You, me and probably everyone else.

Richard   This ought to be depressing me but it isn't. I suppose it is all right to be human and all this is about being just human. God knows that. It doesn't mean that we have to be stuck in the same place going round and round in circles, though that's what we often choose. What's exciting here is that we are really clearing some ground, exploring, maybe maturing as well.

Brice   Where do we go now?

Richard   We're ready to have a look at the message of Jesus. What he really said and the ways we cope with it, good and bad.

Brice   Mostly bad, I expect.

The Gospel Within the Gospel

Richard   The New Testament is where the things that Jesus said have been recorded, but it is not a systematic narrative. Jesus did not set out to write a three-volume treatise on his understanding of God and humanity. What we have was picked up through the memory, the oral tradition, what people heard him say. For me, the most exciting part of what Jesus said clusters round the parables. He seems to have been a memorable and colourful teacher with a natural genius for illustration. The very word parable means the same as *parabalo:* lasso. Jesus would grab an example, he would lasso something from everyday affairs such as village life or the sequences of nature. He would draw them into a kind of divine interpretation and give them spiritual meaning. The deepest of all his parables seem to be about the grace and graciousness of God.

Brice   And if you had to select just one of the parables for us to look at - you do have to actually - which would it be?

Richard One of the most famous is the parable of the prodigal son, which I actually prefer to call the parable of the gracious father, because the real focus is on the homecoming. The parable is about the fact that God's love is like the love of the father in the story. A love that is unyielding and unconditional. This parable shows two pathological responses to that love: the older brother is trying to earn it or trying to deserve it by working all the hours in the day, and the younger brother is saying, 'My Dad is so soft, I can do anything I jolly well like.' For him God is a mug. He's just a big soft-hearted social worker and he can get away with anything. Each has missed the point, because each has found a way of pushing away the unconditional love of the father. It is too hard to live with this insanity of love, because it appears to require nothing from them.

Brice The older son is making sure, albeit unconsciously, that he has earned his inheritance, the unconditional love of the father. We can see this in the envious and uncomprehending response that he has when his younger and wayward brother is so fêted by the father. But, of course, by earning it he is trying to reduce his own sense of vulnerability. He is trying to take away his father's capacity to give him unconditional love.

Richard 'I've earned it and it's mine.'

Brice By rejecting the gift in this way he is showing his need to control or set limits on the unconditional and gracious giving of the father.

Richard He's made his work a condition of receiving the gift that is free.

Brice The older son has fallen into the 'salvation by works' trap. By diminishing the love gift of the father, to make it bearable, he has also diminished his own opportunity for spontaneous, joyous response. Doing anything for the father becomes a duty and not a joy. He has to think about doing it, he doesn't just find himself doing it and loving it.

Richard   There's nothing wrong with working hard, but this is not a son who whistled behind the plough ...

Brice   No, this is a son who pushed himself on, despised his brother and secretly resented his father. Many of us Christians can slip into this trap. We push ourselves on, despise our fellow Christians for what they seem to have and secretly resent God for giving it to them and not to us.

Richard   Indeed, and this is an illustration, among other things, of Christian rigorism. It seems to me that what we have to do is to try and steer a course between rigorism and irresponsibility in our theology and it is one that we can never get quite right. The temptation is to do what the elder brother did and very grimly try to earn something that we can have simply by asking for it.

Brice   And yet knowing that is so frustrating. When I feel trapped like the elder brother, it doesn't help me just to have it pointed out. A healthy impulse is to look for more.

Richard   The prodigal son seems to have taken the part of the father's gift that was, as it were, transportable, his inheritance - his life - and detached himself from the source of the gift, which is part of the gift.

Brice   So he too found a way of taking control of the gracious, loving, gift. He took it and separated himself from the giver. The prodigal reduced his sense of vulnerability to the father by simply up and leaving. What is so powerful here is that his inheritance, the thing that he so desperately wanted, becomes worthless to him when he leaves home ... He doesn't really know what to do with it ... He tries to buy the thing that he already had but has fled from: love. In trying to gain control of love, he loses it.

Richard Another illustration of our human condition. When the prodigal had lost everything he gained a tiny notion of how great and unconditional his father's love for him actually was. Thankfully, that was enough to drag him home.

Brice The prodigal illustrates the irresponsibility that you referred to but he is also all about passion. This was the son who had access to his passions. But he seems to have believed that his passion was unwanted. So he left.

Richard This is a beautiful parable about God's love for us and his ideal relationship with us. For me it is a sort of 'Gospel within the Gospel'. If we lost everything in the New Testament and had this parable we would have the Gospel. Youngsters come to me in their anguish and guilt because they're worried about being sent to Hell. They believe that they haven't got the formula right. They think that they are not believing in the right way or that they are not believing the right things. They've either been in the far country wasting it, or they've been trying to follow this rigid kind of hyper-religiosity. All in the face of this extraordinarily gracious God. Gracious to both sons. It seems to me that here Jesus' message is at its most clear. In this parable, this metaphor, Jesus is addressing humanity's big problem: our problem of meaning. We don't know the nature of this God whom we suspect exists or passionately believe exists and with whom we want a relationship. We don't quite know whom we are relating to. Jesus puts content into this vague picture. He says, 'God is gracious and loves you unconditionally.' But, like the sons in the parable, we seem to find it too hot to handle. Here we all are going around in our little prison houses; afraid of God, afraid of each other, and afraid to take risks. And yet the beauty of Jesus' picture of God is that he gives us permission to mess it up a bit, to fail. We don't have this forbidding parent looking over our shoulder saying, 'If you wet your pants you are going to sleep in them all night.'

Brice   Even though a lot of us would like to think we do.

Understanding Our Splitness

Richard   We've looked at this parable and seen that it is not just the story of these two boys; something is going on at a deeper level that reflects our own muddled response to the ideas, person and experience of Jesus. I've found your psychologizing helpful. Is there more?

Brice   Perhaps this parable is telling us about a split that exists in all of us. It also seems to imply that God is rather interested in helping us with it.

Richard   Go on.

Brice   The states of mind represented by the two sons are, I think, present in all of us all of the time. We just might not be aware of it.

Richard   You mentioned a split. What do you mean?

Brice   A split between the search for self, passion and personhood in the prodigal, and a search for holiness by the older brother. Neither of these searches is going on in the secure and empowering knowledge of the unconditional love of the father. Instead, they are happening on the basis of having diminished, controlled and rejected it. Furthermore, at first sight they appear to be mutually exclusive: the older brother despises his younger brother and his younger brother has to leave home. They don't attempt to share the inheritance. And so it may be in us, because splitting, it will come as no surprise to you to learn, is a form of defence. It is an unconscious process designed to split ourselves in two. We call one bit good and the other bad and dump the bad bit, usually into someone else. The payoff for this very human foible is to create a sense of order out of what feels like unmanageable chaos and conflict. This process is like an overenthusiastic spring-clean and it makes us stuck.

Richard Why?

Brice We've thrown out things we needed to help us to mature. The split must be healed to get these parts of ourselves back.

Richard So once again, the defence that protects also imprisons. What is the defence against? Give me an example.

Brice Okay. Example. We are talking here about the artificial but apparently compelling need to separate our intellectual human abilities from our human passion. The effect is to turn passion into something that is perceived as dangerous, destructive, unspiritual; or to turn the spiritual journey into a kind of grotesque hyper-religiosity where a kind of self-righteous fervour counterfeits and replaces our passion.

Richard Sex is part of our passionate ability. What about that?

Brice We are fundamentally sexual beings but, for many people who try to follow the God that Jesus points to, that sexuality is feared and denied in themselves. It is perceived as working in opposition to their spirituality: it has been split away from the part of themselves that they regard as good and projected into others who are perceived as deviant, hysterical, loose, morally corrupt or lascivious. Anger is a further example. Anger is an expression of our passionate selves and yet many of us attempt to deny our anger; we believe it to be in opposition to holiness. All our feelings and felt reactions are part of our passionate ability. Some Christians try to split them off from the rest of themselves in an attempt to make the confusion and chaos that is part of our spiritual journey logical and understandable.

Richard But we are not then whole people: we are half-people.

Brice From the viewpoint of the prodigal brother we get an equally tragic picture. This is of the person who despises the spiritual journey because it is linked, in themselves anyway, with a feeling-crushing and over-intellectualized approach to spirituality. They manage this by splitting it off from their passionate selves and go off to search angrily and sensually for their personhood, their meaning. People in this predicament rarely find what they are looking for. Nevertheless, they believe, sometimes correctly, that the Church is worse than useless to them: it embodies everything that they want to get away from.

Richard Obviously the Church is a bit of a sitting duck for this one but it often asks for it.

Brice And yet, it does seem as though God offers, in this parable, a way of bringing these two split halves of ourselves together. Unfortunately, it is one that is too frightening for us most of the time and so we behave as though the possibility doesn't exist. Indeed, as we saw in the previous chapter, the human parts of our institutions make it harder to bring our spiritual ability and our passionate humanity together. In this discussion we are seeing how, inside ourselves, in the little vessel, the little temple, we create an unconscious environment where it is equally hard.

Richard   Because of this splitting thing?

Brice   Yes.

Richard   From the way that Jesus has drawn the old man in this parable, we can conclude that he is patient and non-judgmental towards both his sons. His love for them both was unyielding and unconditional. And the implication of what you are saying is that if we Christians can be more confident of that love, more secure in it, then we will be able - feel safe enough - to allow our passion and our rationality to meet. Our ability to feel and our ability to think. And for that to be the context in which our spirituality matures.

Brice   Yes, but it is terrifying. The meeting of the inspirational love of God with the natural spontaneity of man.

Richard   Anything could happen . . .

Brice   Anything would happen more for more people if we hadn't created institutions that so often interrupt the process by obscuring the message of Jesus. Worse than that, our churches often actively, if unconsciously, maintain the split in us. Many of us have an inner world that is so founded on all the defences that we have talked about, including this splitting, that it is very hard for us to do more than momentarily experience our spontaneity. For that spontaneity to be available to the inspirational and unconditional love of God we need to take risks.

Richard　So what do you suggest we do?

Brice　It's more a case of what we might be able to stop doing. In our inner worlds and in our churches we can let something more creative and godly happen. You see, most of the things that we have been discovering together are things that churches, and people in churches, do that simply spoil things: they get in God's way. Where we need to go next in this discussion is to see how your understanding and wisdom on spiritual growth and my making plain that which was previously in the unconscious - against all the odds of institutionalized denial - can be combined to help us stop doing things which interrupt and undermine our relationship with God.

Richard　Well that's certainly the great struggle of Christianity and it happens very powerfully on an individual level too. Perhaps this would be the moment to look at one of the great facts of our faith. Sin.

Sin

Richard　I'd like to hear a shrink's definition of sin, because it is probably the only really empirical Christian claim, the claim that we are fallen. It is one of the few things we can actually demonstrate. We can't demonstrate the resurrection and we can't demonstrate the existence of God, but we can, only too easily, demonstrate the fact that there's something screwed up about human beings. And we have a particular theological angle to that. We call it sin.

Brice The notion of sin has been turned into a sort of religious commodity and used and abused for a long time. A basic sort of core meaning, as little obscured by human artifice as possible, might be hard to arrive at.

Richard The shrink covers his exits. I've got to push you anyway. It is important, I think, because sin is probably the right word, metaphor, whatever you like, to understand what it is that sits so powerfully between us and God.

Brice Perhaps it's helpful to consider sin as stemming from a kind of fear: a fear of intimacy with God. We have just been talking about the effect of this fear in the context of our own splitness and how that limits our natural spontaneity. If the ingredients for spontaneity are kept separate then the availability of fertile ground for the inspiration of God to catch on, like a seed, and grow is limited. The other part of this, and it is a striking paradox, is that there is a deep insecurity in us that stops us from letting the split heal – we lose control. It is that sense of fragmentation, disharmony, whatever one calls it, that we all know and that we desperately want to move on from.

Richard That God beckons us on from . . .

Brice Often we can't go because, to a greater or lesser extent, we are stuck in the most aching of human predicaments. We want something very badly, but feel too insecure to let go of the things that we have created for ourselves which, although briefly taking the ache away, get between us and what we want. From a Christian shrink's perspective, this is the basis of sin. Now, what we immediately think of when we hear the word sin is not this, it is things like adultery, stealing, swearing, lying etc. I don't think these are sin as such but rather the product of our struggle to try and circumvent the blockage caused by this sin thing. They are the symptoms of the disease: the spots on the skin that tell us that the virus is there; they are not the virus itself.

Richard Can you take that further?

Brice Let's think what happens when we divinize metaphors, sanctify language and fundamentalize the chaos of our inner worlds. We impose institutionalized moral strictures on each other or try to make ourselves godly by repressing our personhood and splitting parts of ourselves away. What we are doing, when we do this, is attempting to thrust through this thing that separates us from God. Although our intention is good, we are hanging on to our need to be in control, and we fall pathetically and destructively short of union with God. We get frustrated and angry with God for not helping us when all the time he is there ready and available. Like the father in the parable.

Richard This is interesting stuff. One of the words for sin in the Bible is an archery term meaning to aim for the target but to miss. It is describing sin as springing from a natural inclination to get it right but an inability to do so. Which leads me on to something else that you have just given me a new angle on. Why we do what we would rather not do. I know the right thing to do, it is rarely ignorance that is my problem. The real problem is a will problem not a know problem. We know what the right thing to do is, but there is something perverse and destructive that leads us, often against our own best joy, to oppose it. There is both a compulsive wilfulness about it and a helplessness. There is something about human nature that is not complete: we are on the way, we are still developing. What you've said about that so far is fascinating and liberating. There is something about sin that reflects the presence in us of a wholesome struggle. Some theologians talk about the basic human problem as being that we are in a fallen state, we were once perfect but we fell from that. I think that's no longer adequate and tend towards the idea that we are maturing creatures, we are children staggering into the light, growing up, experimenting with right and wrong. However you theologize it, the Christian doctrine of human nature is that it is tragically flawed. We are incapable of achieving our own visions, our own goals. We muck up our best institutions. We muck up marriage, we muck up human community and we muck up ordinary human relationships.

Brice So, no chance of Utopia then?

Richard You can almost predict that any blueprint for a perfect society that you conceive and manage to institute would shipwreck on this insane characteristic. Our ability is constantly undermined by our insecurity. I'm fascinated by the way we seem to sabotage ourselves, both as individuals and as institutions. Can you help any more with the notion of sin in this way? I suppose it is an interface of psychology and theology and something you might have an angle on.

Brice Sure, let's return to the splitness and look at it again. We are dealing with a linguistic metaphor to try and com-municate and understand something much deeper. Nevertheless, I think it is intuitively reasonable to imagine that if there is a split inside us, which holds apart bits that we are afraid of letting come together, then there must be a space between them. A sort of psychic vacuum or emptiness. It is too trite to say, as some do, that this is a God-shaped hole. However, there is some use in this idea if we consider that part of the message of Jesus is that God is waiting to fill that gap. He wants to bring the split parts together.

Richard   John ten: 'I have come that they might have life, and have it to the full.'

Brice   And sin is a way of trying to fill that gap and stop the ache. It is a way of coping with the absence of God within and gives rise to so much of our self-defeating activity. The problem comes every time we try to make this thing work and fit. In an effort to cope with the unacceptable knowledge that it doesn't, we expend our psychic energy in mounting defences against anything that challenges this state.

Richard   Small wonder, if this is going on, that our spiritual institutions often work against people gaining a healing knowledge of God.

Brice   It is interesting that the sins that are seized upon with such vigour tend to be those that are to do with the gratification of human passion: sex, anger, greed, things like that.

Richard   A special kind of condemnation is reserved for these passionate mistakes.

Brice   Perhaps this response comes from people and institutions that have split off their passion and denied it and repressed it and are looking for some poor hapless soul to project it into. It's a great way of deflecting attention from their own shortcomings. But I ask you: who are the greater sinners? Jesus was compassionate to the passionate but deeply angry with the hypocrites.

Richard   The psychiatrist oils his barrels.

Brice   Well I just hope that this book will make it harder for that sort of hypocrisy to go on happening. I mean, I hope it will illuminate some of the ways in which we lose, undermine or otherwise mess up the opportunities for people to get to know God better.

Richard And that's what the next chapter is about, right?

Brice Right. In the next chapter I think we will find ourselves continuing these themes. But first a little light relief.

Games Christians Play

Brice Let's lighten up for a bit and talk about some of the games we are given to playing.

Richard Such as?

Brice 'Durham Challenge', 'Mine's Bigger Than Yours', and 'Ill Be Your Pope/Shepherd'.

Richard Start with Durham Challenge, how does that go?

Brice Durham Challenge is an easy game to play. The idea is that you avoid a difficult issue by concentrating on one that is, in some way, associated with it but that is much less distressing for you or the group you're a member of. It is called Durham Challenge because the challenge embodied in the game, namely to find the most irrelevant thing to concentrate on in the most distressing situation, was perfectly illustrated a few years ago by the then Bishop of Durham, the forces of nature and a lot of people who wanted to play this game.

Richard The Bishop of Durham said that he wasn't convinced that the virgin birth really happened and caused a hullabaloo thereby . . .

Brice That's right, and whatever else you think about it, it was a valuable hullabaloo because it got people talking. A little while later, however, York Minster was hit by lightning, caught fire and was badly damaged. Talk then became centred around whether or not God had struck the minster out of wrath for the bishop's doubts.

Richard Utterly silly. If God had wanted to zap the bishop he wouldn't have missed, and what's he doing zapping honest Christians when he could rub out a few genuinely evil people instead? Drug barons and the like.

Brice Nevertheless, it served its purpose for those who didn't want to face their own doubts about the virgin birth or, perhaps, anything else. Shame really, because exploration of our doubt is the path to greater faith.

Richard Does Durham Challenge have a psycho equivalent?

Brice Yup, we call it displacement. If we find something too anxiety-provoking we displace the emotional energy it contains on to something that doesn't matter so much, something we are free to get heated up about. You see it a lot in families that are coming apart at the seams where fierce, bitter arguments occur over the most trivial matters.

Richard It doesn't just happen in families. Committees and church councils all know about this one.

Brice Another example is the debate that sprang up a while back about whether or not HIV is God's punishment meted out to homosexuals.

Richard If that's the case, why don't lesbians get it?

Brice   There are responses to that, none of them particularly useful, but that's not the point of this game. You see, banging on about punishment from God is Durham Challenge to avoid distressing questions about suffering and homosexuality.

Richard   This all puts me in mind of something rather similar. I call it Associational Sacralization.

Brice   Not, I posit, a particularly elegant expression.

Richard   No, but one used to describe a common phenomenon.

Brice   Proceed.

Richard   It happens when we sacralize, make too important, the incidental or accidental factors that accompanied important moments in our life or faith. The life of Jesus provides us with a good example. For Christians, Jesus is the incarnation of the divine mystery. Through him we have discovered the true nature of God. That is the central Christian claim. But Jesus was also a first-century Jew. How many of the characteristics of his world do we treat as important? I don't believe there are many we should bother about, but many Christians disagree. For instance: women were subordinate to men in Jesus' day and the early Church more or less maintained that tradition.

Brice   You could say the same thing about slavery.

Richard   You could, and it took the Church a long time to acknowledge that the social norms of Jesus' day were not binding on them. Nevertheless, it is a great danger for a certain kind of mind. We want a kind of absolute security, to be told what to do and think. We find freedom too great a responsibility so we set up these highly detailed systems that programme our lives in every way. We end by making irrelevant things sacred, sometimes immoral things. And because they were done that way in Jesus' time they must be done that way today. It's a fear of time and change and the responsibility they thrust upon us. Many of the debates that disfigure the Church today are about this issue, the inability to separate the essentials from the incidentals.

Brice It's not hard to see how Associational Sacralization can feed Durham Challenge. Incidentals are so useful when essentials threaten.

Richard What's the antidote to Durham Challenge?

Brice Identify the issue that is being avoided and keep asking about it. You get Durham Challenge played in all sorts of situations. Decision and planning bodies and Bible-study groups for example. I remember being at a meeting to sort out the regular cleaning of a building which was always dirty. We spent ages discussing where the equipment should be kept in order to avoid the real, and much more painful, issue which was that someone was lying about doing it when it was their turn. Let's move on to another game. I call it Mine's Bigger Than Yours. It is the way we try to convince ourselves of something by giving it special names. It often shows itself in the language we use. When we are playing this game we speak a sort of Zionese.

Richard Give me an example.

Brice 'The Lord has given me a word for you,' or, 'I took God into the situation.' Those sort of things. I think that sometimes we want something so much that we try to force ordinary things to be special. We want to be more than we are. We try to make God dance to our tune. It often contains a sort of arrogance that belies our underlying insecurity.

Richard This sort of thing sometimes comes across as a bit phoney. Especially to outsiders: people not of the culture.

Brice For the simple reason that it sometimes is phoney.

Richard When someone tries to play Mine's Bigger Than Yours, what could I say? What's the antidote?

Brice You could respond with something like, 'I'm sorry, but I don't quite understand what you mean by that.' If the person trying to play this game is really saying, 'I want to interfere here and if I dress it up in spiritual-speak then I will be listened to and thought holy', then they will be suitably confounded. If, on the other hand, they are in a position to be helpful, they still can be. You must have come across this game all over the place.

Richard I have, and I wonder if what might be behind this is disappointment in the ordinariness of things. I came across a name for it once.

Brice Big words coming, everybody . . .

Richard It's called the Routinization of Charisma. Everyone is familiar with the experience of coming down from a high to dull normality and it takes considerable maturity to deal with it. For instance, most marriages or committed relationships begin passionately. We call it 'being in love'. It is a delicious state of temporary insanity.

Brice Insanity?

Richard I call it insanity because its main characteristic is an idealization of, and an absorption in, the other. Some people sustain this intensity their whole life long for some reason or other, but most of us come down, though not necessarily with a bump. We discover that loving a person or being in love with them does not miraculously rescue us from the normal wear and tear of human relationships. We have to learn how to get on with ordinary routines together. We have to adjust and learn to live with the other person's ways. We acknowledge that we, too, are not perfect. Immature or naïve people do not make these adjustments easily. They thought it was all going to be like a fairy tale romance and it's turned out to be about getting on together. The same thing happens in movements and institutions. They often start as the result of a great vision and their early phase is characterized by excitement and success and the unifying power of a common purpose. But this phase cannot last. Ordinary human nature is bound to intervene and when it does it can come as a great disappointment and lead to crippling nostalgia. The sociologist Weber called this emergence into unavoidable reality the Routinization of Charisma. Trace any great movement in art, politics or religion and you will see the phenomenon at work. You can actually see it in the pages of the New Testament and in Christian history itself.

Brice   Our lack of maturity makes it hard for us to accept when life is simply life. We try to create intense life experiences instead of experiencing life intensely.

Richard   But so often we wish for the intense personal experience. Many of us have had intense religious experiences, moments of conversion or deepening. We stay 'up' for days, sometimes weeks. Inevitably, the world rolls back into place, routine takes over, the excitement fades. It can be a period of letdown. We can even feel like giving up completely, or we can say yes to reality and recognize that we live in a muddled world that we can make a difference in but only slowly and with many setbacks. That's when we need to summon our courage and our sense of humour and go on going on.

Brice   Right, so much for Mine's Bigger Than Yours. How about I'll Be Your Pope, or depending on your orientation, I'll Be Your Shepherd?

Richard   Sounds juicy, how does it go?

Brice   You'll know this one. It's one where we mistake Christian fellowship for a short cut to genuine human intimacy. The two often coexist, but they are different. People who play this game can't or won't tell the difference and they crash around making a pain of themselves. 'We are one in Christ so I know you won't mind if I just say . . .'

Richard   Too right I mind, if it's none of their business. But, why do you call this one I'll Be Your Pope or Shepherd?

Brice   Because it is played by people who think they have some sort of divine right to tell others what to do and think. They are looking for people to play along so that they can feed off them. These people are often hysterics who need to put their hooks into others and tweak them. It's pretty offensive actually.

Richard   What's the antidote?

Brice   The thing to remember is that hysterical types are often very perceptive, they'll spot your Achilles heel a mile off. Trouble is that they are so self-absorbed that they can only put their insights to destructive use. Their motivation is to get you on to their hook, like a fisherman. They don't want to help you. Not really. This all means that, unless you learn to notice it first, the hook will slip in and only hurt when it is yanked and because they've got a point it will be hard for you to give them the brushoff.

Richard Why do I need to give them the brushoff, and how can I do it in a way that helps them?

Brice Okay, good questions, glad you're following. You need to give them the brushoff because they are parasites, and like parasites they want to use you to make more of themselves. Interestingly, the way you help is the same as the way you get the hook out.

Richard Which is?

Brice Not so fast. Let's see the colour of your money.

Richard Talk, Quack, this crook's loaded . . .

Brice So I've heard. The trick is either to stay quiet and smile, while working out what, if anything, that they have said is of any use, or, and this is much better, say something like, 'That's interesting, I'm just trying to work out how much it tells us about me and how much about you, what do you think?'

Richard I like that. It's firm and it's real. The talking can start. This antidote illustrates something else and that's how to be confrontational in a way that also invites the other person to stick around and maybe grow a bit.

Brice Yes, when we are brave enough to be straight with each other, it must be like this. But we must be gentle, there is no excuse for using confrontation as a weapon.

The Unbearable Feeling
of Stuckness

Our Own Stuckness

Richard In the last chapter we explored the various ways in which we, as individuals, are compelled to repeat things that undermine our maturing process. We discussed the sense of stuckness that pervades many of our church activities and we thought about language, fundamental thinking, internal splitness and sin in this context. The recurring theme seems to be that there are many choices for us to make but that a kind of block often stops us. What's going on in a stuck situation?

Brice Usually it's unacknowledged conflict, either within the individual, between individuals or between groups.

Richard   What would be an example of each one?

Brice   An example of the first is something that we are getting quite familiar with now: the conflict between what we actually feel, want or need and what we believe is acceptable to feel and desire. Conflict between individuals in the church setting is very likely to be an ideological conflict. If two people have very different standpoints on something, and try to have a relationship without the differences being acknowledged, then there will be a part of their shared garden that remains for ever barren. Conflict between groups can be very powerful, especially if they are coexisting in an environment short of human and material resources. It is in this sort of situation that envy and competition may be endemic.

Richard   But unacknowledged?

Brice   But unacknowledged. As is often the case where unpleasant emotional material is concerned.

Richard   I want you to expand on your definition of stuckness.

Brice   Okay: stuckness is going nowhere. Our going nowhere might involve plenty of activity and general thrashing about, but frustration at our lack of progress may be the only tangible result. Some sort of conflict is sure to lurk at the bottom of it. Conflict between some feeling or desire that we have, and want to express, and the belief that the expression is unacceptable. The effect of this unconscious process is to cause us to feel great anxiety, which we may deny, when the unacceptable thought or desire tries to surface.

Richard   What causes the anxiety?

Brice   Fear of the consequences of giving in to the impulse. If the levels of anxiety are at all high, they will become too much to bear and, as we have already seen, we will mount a defence against the unacceptable impulse or feeling so that it remains hidden from our conscious awareness.

Richard   Is it denied?

Brice   Denied, repressed, split off from the self and projected into another, or its opposite feeling could be manufactured. In short, we try to keep the lid on the real feeling.

Richard   I think you call that last example, the one of having the opposite feeling, reaction formation. Why are we so stuck when we are like this?

Brice   Because we are locked into a set of circular journeys which, from within, we are compelled to repeat over and over again. Little vicious circles if you like. For example take sadness. If there is a conflict inside us between what we, deep down, feel about something and what we, at a slightly less deep down level, believe we are allowed to feel about it then we will be stuck. Think of two waiters in a restaurant. One is pushing on the swinging door to get into the kitchen whilst the other is pushing from the other side to get out. The door isn't moving. They are stuck. How-we-really-feel is wanting to get out of the kitchen with the chef's set menu of the day, and it's sadness. At the same time, how-you're-expected-to-feel is on its way in with a list of what the customer expects to be fed. In this case the customer wants happiness.

Richard   The customer being the parents?

Brice   Initially, yes. But the child very quickly learns to internalize or ingest its parents' injunctions. The injunctions soon feel as if they are coming from the child's own self. This then creates the illusion in the individual of internal consistency: 'This is me, this is how I really am'. So we hear people – ourselves even – say things like: 'Sad? No, I never get sad', or 'Angry? No, there's never any point in that; it doesn't help'. When people say things like that they are telling you their life story. At least, their life story so far.

Richard Unpack that a bit for me.

Brice 'Sorry, sir, sadness is off: we don't have the ingredients for that'. This is the defence of denial. 'Sorry, madam, we don't do anger any more, we've had too many complaints, I can offer you some overtolerance instead, and while it's being prepared perhaps you'd like to wipe your shoes on my face?' This is the defence of reaction formation. The person who is too good to be true. Now, until something interrupts this, the individual who has been programmed to respond in this way will be stuck going round and round doing it over and over. We call it the compulsion to repeat and it's very powerful.

Richard How does it work?

Brice Something you are doing makes me upset; I don't like it and I want you to stop. You don't seem to realize that you are hurting me, so I must let you know I'm upset in a way that you can't mistake. I become enraged with you. Problem: my rage scares me terribly – and I'll explain why in a minute – so my anxiety levels go through the roof and a complete loss of mental functioning feels imminent. To stop this happening one of my tried and tested defences is selected by my unconscious and activated. In this case it is that of reaction formation. A set of well used reasons for letting you off the hook will come into my awareness to allow me to *not* have my rage. I'm tolerant and forgiving instead. I unconsciously bury my rage to make my anxiety levels drop. I feel better and I feel virtuous. This can happen in a second or two or take weeks of agonizing. The trouble is that I'm trapped into continuing to be the sort of person who doesn't get angry. Subtly, and not so subtly, I invite you, and others, to abuse me so that I have a reason to keep the defence going. The hidden need is to go on being virtuous and forgiving. If I give it up I will have to own up to my rage and if I was made to feel ashamed of my rage when I was a child . . .

Richard You won't want to own up to it for fear of being rejected. It is back to what you said about things that helped us survive becoming prisons that stop us growing . . .

Brice So strong is this effect that I may have no conscious notion of my real feelings.

Richard You will strenuously deny that you ever feel enraged about things?

Brice Yes. And yet despite this, the sort of person I have described will occasionally explode. The anger finds a way out. The clue is that the explosion will be about something very trivial. Thus ensuring further humiliation for the person concerned and further reason for them to go on repressing the way they really feel.

Richard Are there other ways in which the rage that is in there can leak out?

Brice Two other ways leap to mind: self-martyrdom and what we call passive aggression. I don't want to drop my thread at this stage so we could find some space for them later. For the moment there are a couple of things I need to explain: the difference between anger and rage and the link between shame and my feeling scared of my anger in the example above.

Richard What *is* the difference between anger and rage?

Brice Anger is a normal human emotion. It is a very basic emotion which lets us know that something is wrong. It's a good thing. For many of us, however, the word anger evokes memories and ideas of what is, more accurately, called rage or even hatred. The difficulty is that they all get lumped together. The way I like to unravel this is to think of rage as the result of fermented anger and hatred as the result of fermented rage.

Richard If anger is basically a good thing then what goes wrong?

Brice Anger gets stored up inside us. For most people the trouble starts in childhood. Children instinctively use their anger to get what they need. If children are hungry and not being fed then their discomfort and frustration will make them angry. Small children usually express their anger by crying. The crying sends out the message: 'Something is wrong here so please do something about it'. When they get a little older all sorts of frustrations come flooding in to their life. Frustrations to do with toys, people, bodily needs and not being able, physically, to do or express things. Instantaneous angry responses will be made, all aimed at saying to those more powerful, 'Hey, something's gone wrong, it's hurting, we need help here'. Now, all this time the children are exploring their emotional capacities. Their feelings are something new, they don't know what they can do, so they have to find out.

Richard It's like picking up a musical instrument I am not familiar with. I will have to experiment to get a sound out of it.

Brice That's a good metaphor because, to start with, you'll make mistakes, you'll make a horrible sound. Now, in the same way that people who are trying to learn a new musical instrument often get banished to a lonely spot until they can play more sweetly, children often get isolated with their chaotic emotional experiments. Sometimes it is even said to them: 'Go to your room until you have learnt how to behave'. Which translated means 'You are not acceptable the way you are; go away and don't come back until you have learnt not to have the feelings that make us - Mummy and Daddy - uncomfortable'. Thus the child equates certain feelings with rejection.

Richard And there is nothing worse than rejection. Please illustrate with examples.

Brice Well, pick an emotion.

Richard Sadness again.

Brice Okay, sadness it is. A child might be shamed for having sadness because it makes one or other of its parents feel inadequate: not a good enough parent. A child might be shamed, and so feel rejected, for experimenting with sadness even though it's a good honest feeling. It is in these first few years that the defences I have talked so much about are built. If I'm sad, I get rejected, I feel unloved, and that's quite unbearable. So when I next feel sad I get very anxious, too anxious to bear. I do something, anything, to get rid of the feeling. I deny it's there, I do the opposite, I pretend it's you that's sad and not me, or I call it by another name - flu for instance - anything to avoid rejection. Of course, to start with, this is in the context of a relationship with the parent or parents but soon we know that the parents get internalized so that the injunction 'Thou shalt not be sad' is carried within us into adult

146 Churches and How to Survive Them

life. The defences necessary to sustain it and avoid the crippling fear of rejection if we ever acknowledge our sadness are taken along as well. With our genitals it is even easier to see the evidence: if, when young, someone's attempts to explore their sexuality were shamed then we might expect them to have all sorts of defences against sexual feelings as adults. With Christians this is well illustrated by the special condemnation reserved for anyone who falls foul of some sexual stricture or other.

Richard What about anger? Before you get all carried away.

Brice Right. In the same way anger, or rather the expression of it, is often shamed back inside us and, in response, we defend ourselves against conscious knowledge of it. Usually we use denial, 'But I don't get angry'. Adults in this predicament – and it is nearly all of us to some extent – get very anxious, as in the illustration above, when something happens to us and the 'there is something wrong here' alarm bell of anger starts to ring. As we have seen, anxiety leads to defences and this is true of anger. But we need our anger intact and operating if we are to progress as people and as churches. We need our anger operating in the here and now not the then and there, which is often the case.

Richard By then and there, do you mean things like: 'I wish I'd said so and so, that would reaally have sorted her out!'?

Brice Partly, yes. Unfortunately by the time anger surfaces as a fantasy response to something that has happened to us, it has usually fermented into rage. Our fantasies are not likely to be about using our anger creatively: they are more likely to be about stuffing the other person up good and proper. Further proof to us, if we want it, that our anger is nasty and must not be let out of the bag. Wrong. We can learn, or more accurately, relearn to experience, and maybe act upon, our anger in the here and now. If we do, we will have made an important step in taking ourselves, each other, and, very excitingly, the grace of God more seriously. We'll come on to that soon.

Richard So we are stuck with our anger because there is a conflict in us between what we actually feel and what we allow ourselves to feel. All happening at an unconscious level. Tell me, what sort of things make us feel angry?

Brice Anything that attacks our sense of self, what I have called previously our personhood. Things like not being listened to when we need to be, not being taken seriously, being told what we are thinking or what we want by people who don't know, having our identity attacked, being betrayed, being isolated by people, having our love rejected and not getting the love we need. To name but a few examples.

Richard And you are suggesting that if we can respond to these things when they are actually happening we will be able to move on from our feelings of stuckness?

Brice Yes. In the three areas that we have been thinking of so far, namely stuckness within ourselves, stuckness between us and others, and stuckness within the Church, there is possibility for change. If we can allow ourselves to return to being creatures of the here and now yet set in the adult context, rather than the context of the frustrated infant, we will be more able to be who we are. We will know a certain peace and we will be agents for change. But, first of all, and absolutely crucially, we must think some more about the split I was telling you about in the last chapter. This will help us understand the stuckness that exists between us and God, and help us to understand a little more why it is so important for us to search for our innate spontaneity.

Richard   That nearly wraps it up for that section but before we go on you were going to explain about self-martyrdom and passive aggression.

Brice   I was, wasn't I?

Richard   You were.

Brice   No way round it?

Richard   Nope.

Brice   Okay then. Self-martyrdom is something that individuals in the congregation do that makes me more than usually sorry for the clergy. It's really an extension, an acting out, of the 'chronic giver' type that I was telling you about earlier. It is the end-stage of the disease. You get these types who join churches, often run by people who are good at starting relationships and not so good on the follow-through. They join and then they throw themselves in at the deep end.

Richard   They seem to be involved in everything?

Brice   That's right. They are desperate for approval, but no matter how much they get it's never enough.

Richard   Why not?

Brice   Because what they get from others they have either earned or squeezed out of them. These people can't hear the spontaneous approval that they crave. They dare not keep still long enough.

Richard   So where does the martyr bit come in?

Brice After a while they give it up and the despair they feel turns to resentment, 'Look how much I've done for this church - most of it unasked - and what recognition do I get? None!' Then up they climb on to their crosses, usually in the second or third pew, where the minister can't miss them, and sigh long accusing sighs all through the service. The sighs say, 'You did this to me, you nailed me to this cross, and I'm not going to let you forget it'. Revenge, that's the payoff.

Richard Clerics do this to their congregations, as well you know.

Brice I did know, but it sounds better coming from you. Do you want the nice doctor to tell you all about passive aggression now, then?

Richard Yes please.

Brice Story. Husband and wife decide to go on holiday. He wants to go on a golfing holiday so he can make a few business contacts, she wants to go to the seaside. He wins. In the weeks leading up to the holiday she happens to leave seaside holiday brochures lying around the house. When they are on the holiday itself the wife suffers from a seemingly continuous migraine which spoils his golf completely.

Richard So, the wife is behaving passively but also very aggressively. She won't stand up to her husband when she needs to, but she can still pay him back when it's too late for them to do anything constructive about the problem.

Brice Hole in one. Before we move on I'll just pop in a church example of passive aggression. In a church I once knew there were certain combinations of PA technician and music group leader that guaranteed an appalling sound during the songs. Funny how a microphone that works one week doesn't seem to the next.

Richard   Time to get back on course I think.

Back to the Split

Brice   We need to take this step by step or I'll get confused. Let's go back to what we were saying in the last chapter about the split between our ability and our passion. Looking at the parable of the two sons, we saw that one son had a certain ability and he put it to use in the service of the gracious father. We also saw that there was something deeply amiss with this lad. The clue is his response to his brother's return. It was not the same as the father's response to the homecoming: the older son was envious of his brother and angry with his father when he fêted him. This son had not accepted the graciousness of his father, the inheritance. He was trying to earn it. So, when he saw his brother returning offering nothing but his thin and contrite self, being given a special welcome and, importantly, being able to receive it, he was envious of him. He was angry with the father because he felt chiselled out of what was his. If he had been able to accept the graciousness of his father then he would have thought and felt like his father did at the homecoming.

Richard   Perhaps he did eventually, we are not told.

Brice   Well, possibly, and that's the sort of point I want to get to next. He should have welcomed this passionate brother back, but he didn't want to know because he had no access to his own passion. The only way he could live with the inheritance was to give up his passion. He moaned about not being allowed to have parties but I don't believe he ever asked his dad if he could have one. That was his stuck place. The prodigal did have his passion up-front but the only way that he could live with his passion was away from the source of his inheritance. He took what he could as a cushion against hard times and went it alone. I think that he didn't believe that there was any place for him with his father; he didn't feel useful enough. The prodigal took his passion and banished himself. And that was *his* stuck place. The two boys in this story demonstrate the way in which passion, if not linked with security – which is the same as feelings being linked with rejection as we saw earlier – is passion squandered. On the other hand, if ability is not linked with certainty – the son who stayed at home is not certain of his inheritance, he is earning his free gift because he doesn't really believe it is his for the taking – it is ability squandered. The son behind the plough is trying hard to end up owing the father nothing. The prodigal is also convinced that he is unwanted the way he is, so he takes what he can and shoves off.

Richard   And we can be both of these at the same time?

Brice   Yes. Of course, it's only one possible interpretation of the story, but I find it helps. Everyone has some splits in their psyche. Nobody grows up without scars. There must always be some split in us. Jesus seems to be the only exception. As for us, parented by an imperfect world, we very quickly find out what is required of us, and what we must do. We use our ability to try to create certainty, we want to make sure that we are not going to be rejected. We also work out, very rapidly, what feelings we are allowed to express and explore and banish the ones that lead to rejection. This way our feelings are linked to the search for security or the avoidance of rejection. Our ability and our passion are in conflict and when this is the case, we are stuck. Two bits of ourselves that should be united are separated, operating independently and pulling in opposite directions.

Richard Like the two people you described trying to have a relationship without acknowledging their differences, or the waiters on opposite sides of the door. There's a barrier in the gap between them. Is the separation ever complete?

Brice Hard to say. If it were then, I suspect, our madness would also be complete. The point is that this disconnection exists in all of us a bit. The disconnection makes growing difficult; it promotes stuckness. Sadly, the opposite is what we truly crave. As E.M. Forster said: 'Only connect the prose and the passion, and both will be exalted . . .'

Richard If I am understanding you right we are getting close to seeing how sin, anger and grace come into all this and where we go from there. First I need convincing a bit more. How do I know that what you are saying is not just the fancy of some half-baked shrink?

Brice Good question, Bish.

Richard I thought so.

Brice Jesus himself is our first stop. The picture we get is of someone whose ability and passion were linked together and fully functioning in the here and now.

Richard We are coming back to Jesus in a minute. What else is there?

Brice Evidence from my own and colleagues' clinical work. We see individuals struggling to reach beyond their imprisoning defences to find their forgotten emotions. Often very painfully, they come to realize that much of their ability as people has been perverted into an unwinnable battle to be something they are not. Think of the healthiest children and observe that their apparent wellbeing is not necessarily a product of wealth or intelligence. Rather, it is a reflection of their parents' capacity to let their children, as they naturally will, explore their emotions and their abilities (and in small children I mean things like screaming and spitting) to the limits.

Richard To the limits?

Brice Yes, the limits. You won't be able to use your arms properly until you've found out how far you can stretch, will you? As passionate beings we will never learn to manage our feelings fully unless we can explore the limits of them in a safe environment. One as free as possible of rejection or judgment.

Richard And that's next.

Grace is God Reparenting

Richard Grace is God reparenting. That's your title, what do you mean by it exactly?

Brice I'm struck by Jesus' challenge to the disciples that they must become like little children to enter the kingdom of heaven. As well as this there is the picture we get of God the Father in the parable of the prodigal and Jesus' response to Nicodemus about being born again (John 3:3). With such material Jesus himself introduces us to a new relationship with God. We know that Jesus knew God as Father or Abba, literally, 'Daddy'. A valid response to this, and the Gospel itself, is that we all get another chance, a spiritual chance, to be reparented by God. God through his grace offers us a chance to rediscover the link between our ability and our passion, to explore our limits and to learn more about our spiritual spontaneity.

Richard My experience is that the Church, when it tries to take over the parenting role, or individuals when they try to take over that role for others, often get it wrong.

Brice It is imperative for us to learn to tell the difference between being reparented by God, either directly or through mediating instruments, and false reparenting by well-meaning, but wayward, individuals or institutions.

Richard Beware the false prophets. It is difficult to accept this reparenting. It is hard to tolerate the split parts coming together: the uniting of what you called our ability and our passion. Just remind me, before we go on, what you mean by ability.

Brice I mean everything that springs from our intellectual ability. In its extent and diversity our ability is uniquely human. Given to us by God. The other thing that marks us out as human is the range of our feelings and our capacity to reflect upon them. This is where I get the intellect/feelings or ability/passion split from. But, to me anyway, it doesn't really make sense until we accept our capacity to be spiritual beings. Spirituality sort of laces everything else together. Or it will if we let it. I don't think that our attempts at bringing our split bits together, our prodigal and our ploughman, can ever really work unless there is some sort of spiritual growth as well. What do you say when people wonder if this growth only happens in Christians?

Richard The Bible doesn't teach, and I don't believe, that the Holy Spirit only works in the lives of believers. The difference is that Christians acknowledge or identify the presence and action of the Holy Spirit in their lives. This means that they are more disposed to be led and healed by the Spirit than others may be. But God's grace is available to anyone who wants it.

Brice Yes, and as you know, I think of God's grace as an offer of reparenting. That is a hard thing for us to accept and go on accepting each day of our lives. We often have to let go of a lot of stuff to be able to come to God as little children.

Richard Many of the parables demonstrate that. What's next?

Brice Sin.

Sin in the Gap: Coping Without God

Brice We discussed in the last chapter, and so far in this one, how sin in the gap promotes the split. We try to manage without accepting God's gift of reparenting. Only God can give us his grace but we can be available to it and this is where our anger comes in. Our frustration is the key: frustration, awareness and God's grace. If we want to get out of any stuck place we must discover the conflict at the centre of the stuckness. If, in ourselves, our passion and ability are too separate we will be uncertain and insecure. There will be a void, a pit, a dark chasm which we will find hard to live with. We find ways of trying to bridge it to bring our split selves together. This is a good description of what good psychoanalysis can do: bridging the gap between our thinking selves and our feeling selves, so that we can be sensitive and spontaneous, can live, if you like, in the here and now. Many of the things we call sins are attempts to bridge the gap. Twisted and deformed, they may only stay in place for a short while but while in progress some sense of completeness will be felt. Sin is often an attempt to mature, but an attempt to mature that goes wrong in measure to the amount that we accept or reject God's offer of reparenting.

Richard So, any sin I can think of will have an element of satisfaction, pleasure, call it what you will, that derives from a link, however brief or tenuous, between my passion and my ability. Stealing, lying, cheating, adultery, cruelty, there is always a fleeting sense of feeling more whole, more alive. But it is fleeting, it is an excitement that does not endure.

Brice Exactly, and maybe this helps us to understand why we go on doing it when we would rather not . . .

Richard Saint Paul said, 'What I want to do I do not, but what I hate I do'. He goes on to say that it is sin living in him that does it.

Brice Sin is always replaced by a worse feeling of emptiness so we are driven to do it again.

Richard Sin is addictive. But there is an alternative if we want it.

Brice Which bring us to the next step on our trail: sin is that which tries to span the gap, create links where there are none. Sin works in a mutton-dressed-as-lamb kind of way, but any reintegration of our persons in this self-managing way can, at most, be second best.

Richard I guess many of your colleagues think psychoanalysis is better than second best.

Brice Sure. And there are those in your game who think psychoanalysis is wicked. After all, psychoanalysis fits my definition of sin in one important respect: it is an attempt to span the gap with a bridge of our own making. The difference is that most of the truths it contains exist independently of the process itself. Understandably, some Christians see psycho-analysis being treated as a religion and fear that it obscures the hearts and minds of its adherents from the grace of God. I suppose it is up to the individual to decide whether psycho-analysis serves or supplants our healing by God. Both groups have a point but this sort of frantic either/or stuff is pretty inappropriate. Indeed, it is rather artful of people to try to draw psychoanalysis and the grace of God into opposition. I believe it to be a false opposition, like that between science and faith. I suppose people do it in order to exclude the one they feel most threatened by. Psychos do it to Christ and Christians do it to psychos. A silly game and a destructive one.

Richard Back to sin?

Brice Back to sin. Back to Saint Paul: 'Who will rescue me? Thanks be to God – through Jesus Christ our Lord'. If we are able to accept God's offer of reparenting then there is the opportunity for us to start again via our spiritual nurture rather than our physical one. When Nicodemus came to Jesus one night it was to try and persuade him to toe the line with the establishment. The Pharisees knew Jesus was powerful and they wanted him on their side. They wanted him to join their cosy power base. Jesus frustrated Nicodemus but sowed the seeds for his salvation by telling him that he needed to be born again.

Richard To be parented spiritually by God, through the Holy Spirit and by other nurturers, such as believers and the Church as a whole.

What Place Anger?

Richard   We now come on to anger. This was your idea, so tell me why it is important.

Brice   Anger is a faithful mediator in helping us to accept God's reparenting. It is also the basis for all the ways in which we can take responsibility for breaking into stuck cycles of sinful second best, either between us and God, or between us and others. It is potentially very creative and yet somewhat unrecognized as such. If we look at Jesus' example I think we see that the truly beautiful meeting of ability, passion and grace is often mediated by anger. Anger, not rage, is a key to some important locks which many of us don't dare to unlock. If we could, some surprising doors might open. Anger is the emotion of 'something is wrong' and is born out of frustration. This mirrors the frustration felt by a child growing up in a world that spoils the natural integration of passion and ability and replaces it with this terrible split I've been describing. Life then becomes an unintegrated struggle to manage two parts of ourselves which cannot actually function separately. Some people try to resolve this by splitting off and pushing away as much of their ability as possible. They attempt to create an illusion of integration. It is as if they have a broken doll and decide to throw all the bits away but one. Of course, what is left is whole; but it is not complete. In the same way it is tempting to wish to be totally passionate, ripping through the world in a whirlwind of emotions and feelings.

Richard   At first one might feel tremendous liberation and a gorgeous sense of abandonment.

Brice   And that's great occasionally. But if we repress our ability we repress part of ourselves and that part turns inwards and attacks our personhood. Like a plant in a see-through sealed case. It will grow back on itself when it meets the invisible barrier. It chokes itself to death. The passionate whirlwind of raw emotion eventually collapses and may lead to complete self-destruction. Think of the prodigal who so narrowly escaped starving to death in a friendless wilderness. The other alternative is to swing right the other way and try to exist with just our ability. This is the son behind the plough. People who think like this tend to mistrust their feelings to the point of attempting to exclude them. Depression often results. If we are fortunate this depression may be the start of our healing. These two extremes are hard to imagine in reality but we all lie between them. If these extremes were better integrated in us we would have more freedom to slide up and down the scale as we needed. We could be all passion one moment, all reason another, and in between in another. And, importantly, each would be firmly in the here and now. We see this most clearly in the child. The child might be squealing with all-consuming joy one moment, concentrating on balancing a toy brick on his sleeping sister's head or, a few minutes later, negotiating with a parent for a between-meal snack.

Richard Where does this ability to function so well in the here and now go to?

Brice Our human parenting fails us because it was never designed to succeed alone. A Christian could be considered as someone who has become frustrated with the stuck second best of sin in the gap. Their anger, their sense of something wrong, has become more powerful than their compulsion to stay stuck and sinful and in that moment, which may be fifty years long, they say yes to God's offer of reparenting. At this moment a miracle takes place. God has given us new life, we are spiritually born again.

Richard Children of God, available to God's offer of new life . . .

Brice A fresh chance to integrate our passion and our ability in the way it was meant to be: in a spiritual context, on God's terms; with God, not in spite of him. This is a good moment to take on board another important part of this process. God's judgment. When we try to manage the gap ourselves, we exclude God, we turn our back on him. His judgment is plain enough in the Bible and it is like a natural law: if you turn your back on me and refuse the parenting I offer, you cannot be my child. For us the offer is there for as long as we are in a position to choose.

Richard And none of us knows how long that is. It is through God's grace that we repent. Why some accept this offer and others don't is a mystery. In any event it is part of a maturing process so we don't expect someone who is being reparented by God suddenly to be completely morally mature, to be utterly holy, to be completely wise and to live permanently in the here and now - to be spontaneous.

Brice No, but the change is underway, and the quality and speed of that change will be affected by how available we are to God's grace, his parenting.

Richard It is this idea of reparenting, and our availability to it, that has so far underpinned our discussions. Next, accepting this notion of reparenting, I think we should look at some ways in which we can be more available to God. Or, to put it another way, look at some of the things that make us unavailable to God.

Growing is a Frightening Business

Brice Growing is a frightening business. If we neglect our ability to understand or our ability to feel it is going to become harder for us to grow in holiness, become more like Jesus. Nevertheless, God undoubtedly uses those of his children who feel compelled to memorize endless Bible verses to the exclusion of their inner emotional distress. In the same way he undoubtedly uses those who seek to deny any need for reflection or intellectual rigour by trying to live as if every thought that comes into their heads is from God or the Devil, depending on whim. Indeed, the greatest advertisement for the existence of God is that he continues to speak through us and to parent us, muddled though we are.

Richard A lot of what we do undermines our maturing. It affects us and those around us.

Brice The list I made earlier of the sort of things which happen to us all and which should make us angry is useful here.

Richard The things that undermine our personhood?

Brice Yes, and all these things happened to Jesus. Take three examples. His treatment by the Pharisees, he was mocked, isolated and attacked by them. In the temple, prior to throwing the money-changers out, he felt his identity attacked and his message rejected (Luke 19: 39-44). When the bleeding woman touched his coat to get healed she sought to gain from him without being noticed (Mark 5: 25-34). The implication is that she was afraid of him and that made him angry. Jesus dealt with all of these situations in the here and now. He knew something was wrong, he considered it and he acted. Now, fascinatingly, it is not possible to say whether or not he was working on a spiritual level or an emotional one. He was too well integrated. In any event these incidents show, like many others, Jesus as fully alive and spontaneous in the here and now. He is passion, reason and holiness, all at once.

Richard The Bible says that we must be angry but sin not. Having looked at our relationship with God let's extend our discussion outwards to take in those around us. Can using anger in the constructive way you've described help us to cut through some of the stuckness? Thinking of the way of looking at sin that we discussed earlier, tell me what you would expect to see if we are angry and *do* sin.

Brice Anger, where passion and ability are not allowed to meet, results in things like rage, hatred, grudges, gossip, hypocrisy, guilt and shame. In the same passage where we read that sin and anger do not belong together we have the answer: 'put off falsehood and speak truthfully to your neighbour'.

Richard This is where we become agents of change.

Brice We can learn, little by little, to recognize the stucknesses that exist in ourselves and use the creative power of our frustration and anger to repent and become available to God's gift of reparenting. He will replace the compulsion to repeat over and over the denial of parts of our passion and ability with his grace, our inheritance. We will grow towards the perfect integration that Jesus gave us as an example. There's a trap waiting here for us to fall into and it is a very popular one. It has to do with forgetting that our starting point is the way we really are right now and that this is okay with God. Too many of us try to make ourselves acceptable to God, try to change ourselves with grand gestures, rather than accepting who we really are.

Richard   It's pointless because it pushes away God's grace. Like the prodigal's brother. That way we would end up sad and bitter, because it would seem as though God had let us down. In reality we were not letting God be God. So what is the way to avoid the trap, do you think?

Brice   Little miracles. Little steps towards greater wholeness. They are the ones that stick. Now, time for an example or two. Suppose I keep interrupting you when we are talking. It means that you're not being heard, I'm not listening and so you are being diminished by me. If this happens every time we meet then our relationship will be stuck. We might continue to have a relationship but it will not be able to progress.

Richard   Somewhere I'll be getting angry.

Brice   If our relationship means enough to you, you will be frustrated that it is being stuck by me. Now, get this into the here and now and you are ready to help a little miracle come about in my life.

Richard   Your life?

Brice   Sure. What do you think it is like being the sort of person who keeps interrupting people?

Richard   Kind of lonely.

Brice   If you can sense the stuckness between us and respond to your frustration with a little creative anger you might be able to say something to me about it. I have now discovered that you take our relationship, and therefore me, seriously. It's real and it's in the here and now. Suddenly we can do business and we aren't stuck any more. Just as importantly, there are benefits

for us both as individuals. For instance, you might find that
giving voice to your anger has not destroyed our relationship
or driven me to take a load of pills. The security of God's
parentage has made it safe enough for you to bring together
your ability and passion. The benefit for me is that I am
experiencing a little of God's reparenting through you, and that
may help me to grow.

Richard Can you explain how?

Brice I was stuck in a vicious circle. I was compelled to keep
interrupting you because that was how I had learnt to hang on
to people, to stop them going away. Maybe I'd grown up in a big
family where there wasn't enough attention to go round and I'd
discovered that if I was quiet I would get forgotten about. All
my life I've been stuck living as if this were the case. My
desperate flimsy little bridge created to get my ability to
minister to my needy passionate self is talking at you. I am
trying to hold on to you. The tawdry sinfulness here is that, in
trying to get my needs for love met, I am diminishing you and,
furthermore, hindering your love for me. I'm holding on to you,
but at arm's length. We are stuck in a stiff dance.

Richard This reminds me of what Jesus says about turning the
other cheek when we are assaulted in some way. For many
people, turning the other cheek means being a doormat.

Brice That's surely just repressed intolerance turning into a
sort of rage-driven overtolerance. I think that a fresh way of
looking at turning the other cheek is not to pretend it doesn't
matter to us when we are assaulted, that's absurd. Rather, we
can let it be known that it does matter, that we are angry, but
that we will stick around anyway and perhaps sort it out. In
other words: you are angry with me but that doesn't mean our

relationship must come to an end. God's grace working through you can turn my vicious circle into a virtuous one.

Richard This is a picture of how God feels about us and mirrors how Jesus treated his disciples when they let him down, as they often did. Tell me more about how I can help you.

Brice If I am able to hear the message from you that my attempts to abuse you, by pulling you into my personal inner drama, are not acceptable, then two things are suddenly out in the open and can no longer be pretended about. Firstly, I am in a muddle and, secondly, you care about it. These two facts might hit me like a bolt from the blue but interestingly they are God's message to us as revealed in Jesus.

Richard You Brice, you Richard, are in a muddle and I care about you. What next?

Brice You stop me and indicate that my always interrupting you is a problem and that you think it stops us moving on and you want to do something about it. It is now very hard for me to abuse you again in the same way. Between us the cycle is broken, the stuckness is unstuck and potentially that tawdry little bridge falls to be replaced by the true integration offered by God through you. We are drawn closer and I grow in wholeness.

Richard Potentially?

Brice Okay, it's not quite that easy. I've got a choice to make. I can either accept your offer or I can turn it down. Turning it down might destroy our relationship. It would certainly involve me in denying the validity of your anger. You would no longer be available to be diminished by me so I might move on to someone else.

Richard   And that might be your life story until you were ready to accept a little bit of reparenting.

Brice   Exactly, but there's more. You see, accepting what you tell me might involve me in feeling some shame and sorrow. Nevertheless, it would be in the context of a deeper relationship with you and a greater availability in myself to the grace of God. So that sorrow and shame will pave the way to a greater self-acceptance based on a knowledge of God's acceptance of me as I am, my increased availability to him, and your acceptance of me. Here we have another cornerstone of what Jesus teaches us about the grace of God. The word for it is repentance and it puts a lot of people off. Unpack the theology a bit for me.

Richard   Okay, let's see what it means. Literally, it means to think again, or change your mind. When Jesus was baptizing people the Pharisees came up to him and criticized what he was doing. He responded by accusing them: 'Produce fruit in keeping with repentance'. Paul when preaching in the Acts tells us to 'prove our repentance by our deeds'. So the first thing that we can say is that real repentance produces a recognizable change in us. When teaching about forgiveness Jesus says: 'If your brother sins rebuke him, if he repents, forgive him'. And in the letter to the Romans Paul writes 'God's kindness leads us towards repentance'. Repentance is linked with forgiveness and with God's grace. When we know that we are loved anyway and cannot forfeit that love, we can find the strength and security to admit that we get some things wrong, need to reconsider, need to repent. This all ties together when we realize what we need forgiveness for. Forgiveness rejected produces anger and anger produces a choice from God: turn to me and be reparented or choose to go on denying your need of me and ultimately you will perish, you will drown in your anger and anxiety.

Brice   That choice is the same as the one that faces me when you get angry with me for diminishing you.

Richard   If you turn that choice down you turn God down. Of course we all do it, but the little miracles happen as well. The difference is that once we have chosen to accept God's reparenting then that's it, we are his child, we are home again.

Brice   At the heart of every stuck situation, either within us, or between us and God or between us and another person, this choice is the same. As God's grace frees us to live more and more with our ability and our feelings integrated we will be able to tell when we are stuck and be able to respond to God's choice; or angry and needing to offer God's choice to someone else so that our relationship can grow.

Adopted by the Church

Brice   Christians, as the Body of Christ, the Church, carry the responsibility of reparenting each other but the capacity so to do is only in measure to the reparenting that they have accepted for themselves from God. This may be from many sources: Scripture, prayer and other Christians. Whatever the steps, the Holy Spirit has been the agent of God's grace. If we try to reparent each other in our own strength, from our unsorted-out, tawdry, sinful bits, we are going to create problems. In most situations things go wrong for one of two reasons. Either someone is not being reparented when they need to be - they are pushing God or others away and nobody loves them enough to help - or, someone is acting out their unparented defensive drama all over everyone else.

Richard This must be what underpins much of the power abuse that we discussed earlier, especially the part that the victim plays. Looking for reparenting and being drawn into an ungodly version of it.

Brice Churches form round the common desire to be reparented by God. When things go wrong, if we look closely, it will usually be because someone or some group in the church is trying to compete with God. This is where it is once again crucial for us to learn to tell the difference between genuine reparenting by God coming through faithful mediating instruments and well-intentioned but wrong-headed reparenting by someone who lacks the maturity to be a faithful mediating instrument. In this case the attempted reparenting comes from the neediness of that person's flimsy bridges and tawdry sins rather than from their grace-given spiritual passionate ability.

Richard Okay then – what are the telltale signs?

Brice The first thing to say is that it is not all as black-and-white as I am implying: none of us is perfect and none of us is all bad. There are three telltale signs which can be observed when someone, either of us for instance, is out of his depth. They are autobiography, judgmentalism and fruitlessness.

Richard Explain the first one.

Brice Autobiography is best illustrated by a little story. A friend of mine was preaching one day and afterwards someone came up and started to tell him all the things that were wrong with his sermon and what they thought he ought to change next time and some bits were good but why did he leave out this and that. You know the sort of thing. So my friend lets him finish

and then just says 'And what's any of that got to do with me?'
A bit brutal and unsubtle but it is a good story because it
illustrates several things. Firstly, everything this chap said to
the preacher was about himself, it was autobiographical. It was
dressed as helpful advice but it was all his own stuff that he
hadn't thought through properly. Stuff he couldn't quite face
but had to talk about. Second, my friend was being abused and
it made him angry. He realized this and responded in the here
and now. Thirdly, by doing so he was refusing to play the abused
child to this would-be abusing parent. Autobiography is at its
most toxic when it comes from the pulpit and usually it takes
the form of a preacher trying to persuade the congregation to
join him on his personal guilt trip.

Richard We're all suckers for that one.

Brice Because at the heart of it is the fact that we are sinners
who need to be forgiven. But that doesn't give someone who
doesn't feel forgiven the right to try and make me feel as
wretched as him. This is all a distorted sham of God's true
reparenting.

Richard Judgmentalism?

Brice Judgmentalism is the toxic cousin of autobiography.
When we are judgmental of others we are projecting stuff inside
ourselves that we can't face and need to deny. Not being able
to face uncomfortable or even terrifying truths about ourselves
is something we will all have to bear till our dying day. The
temptation to gain relief from the ache in that part of ourselves
we are not yet ready to let God reparent, by dumping it on
others, is sometimes overwhelming. The Bible is, as ever, good
on this one. During the Sermon on the Mount Jesus talked
about judgment: 'Why do you look at the speck of sawdust in

your brother's eye and pay no attention to the plank in your own eye?' he says. Jesus here compares the biggest thing he can think of with the smallest. He knew well what it was like to be the dumping ground for other people's projections and that it stopped people seeing him for who he really was. The same thing happens now. Jesus was a carpenter's son and must have known what it was like to have a splinter of wood in his eye. He must also have known what it was like to stand helpless before his father while it was removed. In the same way if we can bear to be helpless before our heavenly Father, incapacitated by our compulsion to sin, and let him parent us then we won't need to be so judgmental.

Richard I like that. We will be able to see things clearly. And the last thing, fruitfulness?

Brice In Galatians: 'The fruit of the spirit is love, joy, peace, patience, kindness, goodness, faithfulness, gentleness and self-control. Against these there is no law'. This is what we look for in those reparented by God. The contrast between the fruitless and the fruitful Christian is the contrast between death and life.

Richard I'm fascinated by the way your professional language echoes biblical categories. Paul tells us, for instance, that we are children of God 'by adoption and grace'. There is a sense in which we are children of God by our very birth, our creation. However, and for whatever reason, there is something between us and God, something in the way. It may be thought of in developmental terms: we have not grown to full spiritual maturity yet. Or it may be more traumatic: something has happened that has distorted us and our relationships with reality. Both ways of putting it say something true, and this is where the image of adoption or your helpful image of reparenting comes in. I take all this language, your psycho-speak and Paul's theological jargon, to be saying, essentially, that it is never too late to turn towards healing and maturity. The offer is always on the table, the door is always open. We can turn again and be saved. We can admit the truth of our condition, whatever it is, trusting absolutely in God's parenting love. This does not mean, of course, that there may not be pain in the process, but it will be the pain of growth. The miraculous thing is that we can be born again, over and over. God's endless love is endlessly offered to us, God's hand is stretched out in longing towards us, our response is to reach out and take it. Growing up is not easy, but we do not have to stay stunted by the accidents of our nurture. By adoption and grace, by God's parental love freely offered, we are given another chance, another shot at getting it right, or slightly better. This is the most heart-warming thing about Christianity – we have a home to go to and the door is always open.

SUSPENSE

ROMANCE

BIOGRAPHY

MYSTERY, RELIGION, HISTORY, SEX, HORROR, FICTION, DRAMA, REFERENCE

THE BIBLE

No Easy Answers

The Bible

Brice   I saw something on a church notice board that intrigued me: 'Full Gospel Fellowship - A Bible Based Congregation'. As with all things, it was a highly coded message. Decoded, it said, 'Other churches have departed from it, but we stick to the Bible.' Tell me, why do Christians disagree so much about the Bible?

Richard   I think this is one of those areas Bertrand Russell had in mind when he said that zeal was a bad mark for a cause because it was usually the sign of insecurity. No one gets heated up about the two times table, for instance. People get heated and take sides precisely in areas where there is, indeed can be, no certainty. As a shrink you have already given this phenomenon a fancy name. You called it reaction formation if I remember rightly.

Brice Yes, this is an example of it: uncertainty can't be tolerated, so the unconscious buries it under a crust of overconfidence.

Richard Now if we could really arrive at final and undisputed conclusions about the Bible the rows would cease. Since that is unlikely ever to happen, I can guarantee that people will go on disputing about the Bible. Some people will always claim that they and they alone know the truth and everyone else is an apostate.

Brice Apostate?

Richard It's a word that means traitor, someone who has betrayed the game. Others will adopt a lofty and dismissive attitude and claim that they know that the whole thing is a load of old fairy stories.

Brice What's your line on the issue?

Richard As you might expect, it's a complicated one. It's complicated and it's probably unrealizable. I wish people would use the Bible in the way that works for them and not feel they have to disallow other approaches. It's an unrealizable hope, of course, because our attitude to the Bible has an effect on other areas where we are likely to disagree. The Bible gets used almost like an instrument of warfare, a weapon in the conflict.

Brice Give me an example.

Richard Okay. Take the vexed question of the role of women in church and society. Now, women feature prominently in the Bible. Paul, for instance, makes it quite clear in one place that women are subordinate to men. They should obey their husbands and keep silent in church, making sure that they cover their heads in public worship. What are we to make of that stuff? How are we to handle it today?

Brice   I'm waiting to hear . . .

Richard   Well, it will depend on your attitude to Scripture, how you interpret it. The very word 'interpret' is itself instructive. It means to elucidate, make clear, help people to understand. At the United Nations they employ interpreters who are skilled in rapid translation from and into different languages. The implication is that the Bible is a foreign language or a code that is so complicated it needs to be interpreted, made plain. How do we make plain for today what Paul says about women? It all comes back to our basic assumptions. And let me look at that word before moving on.

Brice   Laying the ground carefully eh?

Richard   Yup. That word 'assumption' is very interesting and important. It is not unlike the word 'faith' or 'belief'. It suggests that there are certain things we cannot prove beyond dispute but assume, take for granted, usually for practical reasons. This is where you decided to stand, this is the assumption from which you will operate. Most of us do not examine our assumptions. In fact, we accord them an almost self-evident status and we are puzzled or angered when they are challenged or repudiated. For instance, it used to be one of the assumptions of white Anglo-Saxons that they were superior to all other races. Kipling called it *The White Man's Burden*. They thought they were the school prefects of the whole human race, sent by God to 'civilize' other nations, especially if they were not white. It was a laughable assumption, but it held sway for ages and is still echoed today.

Brice So, I must be careful about my assumptions. Back to the Bible, back to Paul on women. How do we interpret what he said to make it understandable today?

Richard If you assume or believe that the Bible is the infallible Word of God and that every word in it is sacred and inerrant, then you would say of Paul's statements on women that they come direct from God and are to be obeyed. The fact that they run contrary to the way people feel today is beside the point. God's Word must be obeyed and that's that. I don't agree with that line but I have a sneaking admiration for its toughness and refusal to be moved by current opinions. The thing to notice is that it is based on an assumption about the status of the Bible. And there is an inevitable circularity here. How do we know that the Bible is the infallible Word of God? Because the Bible tells us so. But why should I believe what the Bible tells me? Because the Bible tells me so, and so on. We can never get beyond this circle. We decide to believe that the Bible is God's infallible Word and that's that. Though, as a matter of fact, people who claim to act on this assumption pick and choose like the rest of us. They may practise the subordination of women but they do not necessarily give all their goods away, or refuse to retaliate against an aggressor. In fact, this approach is often a way of describing a particular set of values and opinions, usually right-wing, that claim to come from God but are often held on other grounds.

Brice What other approaches are there?

Richard If you find the view that the Bible is the literal dictation of Almighty God hard to swallow, then there are other possibilities. They, too, are based on assumptions and all of them, to a greater or lesser degree, involve us in wrestling with decisions and not simply taking orders. Broadly speaking, nonliteralists would say that the Bible was inspired by God and God's mind can be encountered as we meditate on it. It is inspired by God using human intermediaries, whose thoughts, memories, dreams and visions put us in touch with the presence of God. The Church of Scotland is good on this. It says that scripture 'contains the word of God'.

Brice   That's nearer to where I'm at, but how does it help me to interpret Paul on women?

Richard   Well, it puts a lot of the onus on us. The theory of inspiration makes room for the human element in Scripture. It requires us to be a bit more sophisticated in our knowledge of the formation of the Bible. It helps if we know, for instance, that the formation of Scripture, as we have it today, was the result of a process that took twelve hundred years. It was written mainly by people we know nothing about, and that it was written under very different circumstances from those of today. It is still a powerful authority for us because it puts us in touch with the inspiration of spiritual geniuses and lets us in on the history of a particular people's religious development. The Bible still speaks to us because it engages with permanently important issues. The historian Ranke said that every age was equidistant from eternity. This means that their insights still speak to us and that we should also trust our own insights.

Brice   I'm getting a bit edgy here. Maybe it's my evangelical skirts showing, but, for me, the Bible is the inspired word of God first, and history and contact with spiritual geniuses second.

Richard   If you hold tight, I think you'll find that I'm bringing it together in a way you'll be able to cope with. If we accept that the Bible is the result of a long human process, inspired by God, but undeniably human as well, then we have to commit ourselves to a task of discernment. In this great library of books, with different approaches and different voices, what is of God and what is of humanity? What is eternal and of enduring value and what is of its day and of only historical importance to us? In the case of Paul, we have to locate him in his time and place and acknowledge that many of his attitudes reflect the culture of his time and not the mind of God. This means, I'm afraid, that much of the responsibility lies with us. In the example about women, I believe that Paul was reflecting the social and cultural assumptions of his day and we are not bound by them. Interestingly, Paul is his own best critic. One of his most penetrating insights, from Galatians, was that in Christ all the human barriers that divide us have been abolished, so that there is no longer Jew or Greek, slave or free, male or female. It took a long time to work out the implications of that insight. The early Church wrestled with the first clause only, though it took them a while to admit Gentiles to the Church. It took another eighteen hundred years for slavery to go, and only in our day are we coming to terms with the equality of women. This shows that the Bible offers its own principles to help us discriminate, to make distinctions.

Brice   But doesn't this leave everything to us? Doesn't it make us our own authority? Christians are called to obey God. If we pick and choose what we want from the Bible, how can we claim to be obedient?

Richard   You have put your finger on a central difficulty there and I am unable to offer an obviously conclusive answer.

Brice   Try me with an inconclusive one then.

Richard   Let's start by looking at the word 'authority' that you used back there. The word refers to something that has power over us. In fact, there are two Greek words in the New Testament that get translated as 'authority' in English. The first one means power, naked force, and it's the word from which our word dynamite comes. It is possible for an institution to have authority over us in this way. This is how police states operate. They brutalize their people by making them obey laws they do not consent to in their hearts and minds. The rule here is, obey or else. But obedience in that context is not genuine obedience, it is oppression. Obedience in the biblical, and truly moral, sense is about consent. I acknowledge the legitimacy of the person or law I give my allegiance to. That won't, necessarily, make it easy to obey; but it does make my obedience a voluntary, and therefore a moral, act.

Brice What about the other word for authority?

Richard Strictly speaking, it is the one that ought to be translated as 'authority' proper. There is the sense of legitimate authority not arbitrary power in this word. It is something that we willingly submit to. This brings me to another distinction in meaning within the notion of authority.

Brice I know we'll get to the point eventually.

Richard This distinction is a bit like the one between power and authority. Power compels our obedience by external force; authority wins our obedience by inward assent. Another way of putting this is to talk about extrinsic and intrinsic authority. Extrinsic authority is like our old friend power. It means the authority comes from outside and compels our obedience, or tries to. Intrinsic authority means that the person or institution or piece of writing simply has authority by virtue of itself. It compels our assent by its own integrity, attractiveness or correspondence with our own sense of truth and reality. There's a place in the New Testament where this distinction is applied to Jesus. The writer tells us that the common people heard him gladly, 'Because he spoke with authority and not as the scribes' (Matthew 7:29). It was the scribes who had official, extrinsic authority but the common people didn't hear them gladly, didn't offer them their obedience. No, they offered that to Jesus, who had no external authority. He was a wandering preacher, a layman, but his words had authority, they hit the mark time after time. Their authority lay in their truth.

Brice Right, what you've done is to argue for a reasoned and Spirit-inspired relationship between the Bible and humanity. This is based on its intrinsic authority and our obedience and discernment. Now, are we coming back to the point?

Richard You betcha. The authority of Scripture is its own intrinsic power to compel our consent. We don't obey it or meditate on it because we are ordered to, told it has extrinsic authority, is God's word (we've already been round that circle), but because it compels our assent. It illuminates us, moves us, comforts us, disturbs us. We don't need to be told, for instance, that we should pay attention to the parables of Jesus, because when we listen to them they compel our attention. They have intrinsic authority. As a matter of fact, it was this quality that probably got particular books into the New Testament. The Church had a whole period without a book, with oral tradition before it became a text. So the Church comes before the Bible and itself established its extent and composition. The formation of the New Testament had its ups and downs. The four gospels and the thirteen epistles by St Paul had been accepted and placed on the same footing as the Old Testament round about the beginning of the third century. The other New Testament writings were received later. Doubts persisted about certain books (Luther loathed the letter of James and couldn't understand how it ever got in), and at times some books got in for a period and were then dropped. A council held at Rome in 382 AD gave the complete list of books of the Old and New Testaments as we have them today. But this might never have happened, we might never have had such an authoritative list of books of the Bible, if certain heretical teachers hadn't produced their own lists and dismissed the rest as rubbish. Marcion, for instance, only recognized a version of Luke's gospel and ten of Paul's letters. Inevitably, the Church in opposing what it held to be wrong teaching was forced into establishing what was correct. What is called the Canon of Scripture was established.

Brice   Once again the bad guys forced the good guys to act.

Richard   Yes, but it shows that the Church went along for hundreds of years without the Bible in the form we now have it. Even after it was established as an official text there were very few around and they could only be read by the handful of people who were literate. They were probably all in monasteries.

Brice   The Bibles or the literati?

Richard   Both.

Brice   Okay, so picking and choosing seems to have been the name of the game.

Richard   Yes, but not arbitrarily. There would always have been this sense that the text must carry its authority with it. Though there is an interesting angle here. It was apparently a common literary practice to attach the name of a famous person to a manuscript, to attach some extrinsic authority to it, in order to gain it a reading. Something similar goes on today where well-known writers with an established readership are invited to write introductions to books by new writers. This is why scholars dispute with one another over the alleged authorship of various books in the New Testament. One of the most interesting examples is the letter to the Hebrews. Our Bible claims that it was written by Paul the apostle, but most scholars, including conservative scholars, are certain it wasn't. They base their case on internal as well as external evidence. It is not a very important dispute but it does illustrate the complexities of the matter. By the same token, other letters attributed to Paul are disputed by scholars. What gives the debate about the Bible its excitement is that we are too far from the times and sources to be able to say with absolute certainty what the exact history is. And, as you would expect, all sorts of views are taken and scholars disagree with each other, some taking a conservative line, some being much more radical.

Brice So how are we to handle it all then?

Richard Personally, I believe the test should be pragmatic. Since we are not going to get exact scientific proof of the certainty of any particular approach, you should use the method that works for you but try not to knock down what might be the different approach of your brothers and sisters. If you think you are swallowing it hook, line and sinker (though I bet you're not!) then bless you, may it bring you to God and increase your love for your neighbour. But please don't say or even think that people who come at it from a different angle are unbelievers. There have been many different ways of interpreting Scripture, some of which would seem quite exotic to us today. The best rule in the spiritual life is to make the most of your own attempts at devotion and commitment and not waste energy on wondering about equally good people who may take a different approach. If you want to take the story of Adam and Eve literally and thereby become holy and more loving, I shall bless you. I hope that you will bless me in turn, though I take it as a myth, a way of conveying spiritual truth by narrative. I hope and pray that my approach will also help me to be holy and more loving. That, after all, is always the test.

Brice   I can go along with that except for one caveat. And I hope I'm not guilty of trying to play It's Not What You Said But What You Missed Out with you, but . . .

Richard   What's the problem?

Brice   There are times when the Bible is misused either by groups or individuals. What do we do then?

Richard   We have to decide for ourselves when someone else's use of the Bible is more than just different from ours, when it becomes misleading or positively dangerous to others. But we must be very sure of our ground and examine our motives for interfering.

Hell

Brice   I suspect from what you've said about the Bible and your attitude in general that you don't believe in Hell. Am I correct?

Richard   Yes, though I'll modify my answer in a moment. I believe that Hell is one of those elements in the Bible that we have to treat with caution and place in context. Jesus and the other characters in the New Testament were people of their day. As well as being open in a special way to God's love and knowledge, they were creatures of their time. They believed in a wedding-cake cosmology, the three-tier universe. Earth was in the middle, the place of departed spirits was below and heaven, quite literally, was above. We no longer accept that particular picture of the universe, though we can still use the language in a figurative way, and words like above and below have an important metaphorical power.

Brice But disbelieving first-century cosmology doesn't necessarily mean rejecting the idea of hell, does it?

Richard No, but you have already added a refinement by talking about the idea of hell. Presumably by that you mean some sort of spiritual state and I'm prepared to go along with you on that, because we know that hell, in that sense, already exists. If I go against my own conscience and deliberately sin in some grave way, I immediately plunge myself into a hell of guilt and remorse from which only repentance and confession will rescue me. And sometimes we are not rescued. It is possible to put ourselves into this unhappy state for a long time, possibly for ever. Do you know the novels of Charles Williams?

Brice Who is he?

Richard He was a poet, writer of novels and friend of C.S. Lewis. He wrote a series of metaphysical thrillers in which he showed how the world of the supernatural penetrated or was another way of looking at the natural world. One of his most unsettling novels was called *Descent into Hell*. The main character is a man so evil and selfish, so beyond the possibility of change and renewal, that he descends eternally into the prison of his own boundless ego and is trapped for ever. Now, that is also a picture, a way of talking, but it does suggest that behind this idea of hell there is the human experience of self-damnation, of casting ourselves out of joy and hopefulness by our own stubbornness and pride. That is a very human

experience and it may be an eternal possibility, but it's a far cry
from the mediaeval picture of eternal fire and fallen angels with
pitchforks chucking lost souls into eternal torment.

Brice Where did that idea come from?

Richard Good question. There isn't much idea of an afterlife
in the Old Testament. There is only a shadowy existence in a
grey underground called Sheol. During what is called the inter-
testamental period, a very hard time for the Jews, tougher, more
vengeful ideas developed. At the end of the age God would
reward his faithful servants and punish their persecutors. The
great division would take place at the Day of Judgment, when
every soul would be raised to the Judgment of Hell or Heaven.
That's why in mediaeval prints you see graves cracking open on
the last day and skeletons emerging for their day in court. Jesus
does not talk much about this but he assumes it as part of the
theological furniture of his age. And he adds an interesting
twist. He uses the local garbage dump as a metaphor for
judgment. That's where the fire and the worms come in. In
Mark's gospel he tells us it is better to cut off a hand and save
ourselves than to go, with two hands, into Gehenna. Gehenna
was originally the Valley of Hinnom on the south side of
Jerusalem, where child sacrifice had once been offered to the
god Moloch. At a later date it became the city's refuse dump,
where rubbish was burned. It was a place where the worm did
not die and the fire was not quenched. By the time of Jesus it
had become a metaphor for the state of sinners after death.
When Jesus used the term, therefore, he was doing what he
always did, which was to take the familiar and use it to surprise
us. He pointed to the danger of unrepented sin, major faults in
our lives that grow if they are not dealt with, and he pointed
to the smouldering garbage in Gehenna and warned us, 'If you
do not face these issues in your life you are sentencing yourself

to the slow burning misery of unresolved guilt and the worm of self-accusation.' The trouble with metaphors, which are meant to shock us into awareness, is that the literal-minded can hijack them. They purge them of their shock and surprise and make them into blunt facts - and highly disputable facts at that. Once hell was established as a sort of geographical fact it was elaborated by subsequent generations till it became a complete topography. Hell, set forth in the finest detail, was used very effectively to keep people in line and scare the children.

Brice   Dante's Inferno.

Richard   Precisely. As a shrink, you ought to have a field day with Hell. Certainly, the hell of the Middle Ages used punishments that had all been tried and tested on heretics and sinners.

Brice   I've never been able to believe in a hell such as that portrayed by the painter Hieronymus Bosch, not literally anyway. For me, Hell is a kind of permanent separation from God. Imagine it would be like being buried in a hole and knowing for certain that I'm forgotten. You see, at the moment, if I feel buried in a hole, I'm able to hope for rescue. However, if we say that something is symbolic then there must be a spiritual reality behind it. What is that reality?

Richard   To answer that I must come back to the paradox of Jesus' life and teaching. He was merciful to sinners, exemplified the divine compassion; but he also begged us to be honest about ourselves and seek the help of the Holy Spirit to change our lives. So there was urgency in Jesus, a definite challenge to us to repent, to turn round and mend our ways. The emphasis is on the challenge, the call to us to acknowledge the reality of our own condition and receive the forgiveness and grace of God. He came to persuade us to lay hold of a gift, not respond to a threat. Our state after death will not be a bodily one. We know that we'll leave these bodies to the elements. We, on the other hand, will have enduring life, but what we've made of ourselves here will presumably affect the way we are there.

Brice   In what sense? I presume you are not suggesting that the wonderfulness of heaven will be dictated by how wonderful we've been as people?

Richard   No, I mean in the simple decision that lies at the core of the Gospel. What we make of ourselves depends upon our response to the fact that God is gracious and will receive us as soon as we turn to him. That may leave hell as a possible state of enduring self-torment, a sort of endless sulk. If it exists like that, however, I suspect that it's more a transit camp than a permanent habitation. If I see you there, I'm sure we'll both be just passing through.

Brice   Either the sulk is endless or it's not.

Richard   In theory, I suppose the sulk could be endless, but it is our choice. The door of the prison has been unlocked. If I choose to stay behind bars for ever, it's up to me. But God is guiltless.

Morality

Brice   You mentioned morality when you talked about hell. Is there a specifically Christian morality?

Richard   Actually, I didn't use the word morality. I talked about sin, certainly, and honesty and the need to acknowledge our true state, our real condition. All that is related to morality, but is not quite the same.

Brice What's the difference?

Richard Well, one has to do with us and God, the other has to do with how we relate to one another.

Brice There is a distinction here?

Richard Yes, and it's an important one. Moralities come and go, change, develop and often repudiate previous moral traditions. We have already thought about some examples, such as slavery. It seems extraordinary to us that our sober, God-fearing forebears were slave-owners or traders. It took a mighty effort by the powerful evangelicals of the Clapham Sect to end that particularly gross evil. We could cite many other examples. The point I'm making is that moralities do change - the very word comes from the Greek for custom, and we know how customs change - and to be too tied to any one system may prevent us from responding to the new challenge that is before us. Moralities, in other words, are practical systems for managing the untidy realities of human relationships. Behind morality is the abstract area we call ethics, which is the study of the principles on which we base our moralities. Scholars debate whether there is such a thing as a specifically Christian ethic. They point to the fact that many of the standards we have inherited come from Judaism and within the moral systems of the cultures of Our Lord's day were common elements, such as the Golden Rule, about doing to others only what you would have them do to you. The contribution of Jesus seems to have been a particular tenderness towards sinners and anger at cruelty and hypocrisy. When asked which was the important commandment, he told us to love God and our neighbour as ourselves. That leaves us with hard questions about how to love our neighbour and what it might mean in particular situations.

Brice   What about the Sermon on the Mount?

Richard   That's the real bombshell. In the Sermon on the Mount Jesus took conventional morality and turned it upside down. He told us to love our enemies, bless those who curse us and give to those who ask, without question. He heightened the moral demand to such an extent that scholars aren't quite sure what to make of it. Was he saying the distance between our bourgeois morality and real holiness is so wide that we should fall on our knees and confess our failure? Or was he setting forth a kind of absurdist morality, so high and extreme that it would make people realize that they had not begun to understand the nature of God? Or was it a definite programme of conduct for his followers? There is little evidence that Christians have tried to follow it to the letter, except for a few saints. I have to confess that I don't follow the Sermon on the Mount, though I do try to let it influence my behaviour.

Brice   So how would you characterize Christian morality?

Richard   I would say it acknowledges the wisdom of the best, and therefore most general, moral traditions of humanity. Care for the weak and for strangers; regard for our neighbours and a concern for their wellbeing. All of this will have negative as well as positive sides. Loving your neighbour means you won't rob him or steal his wife or hurt his children. There is a common thread through the best moral traditions and Christians take hold of it, but they give it a particular twist. The practice of forgiveness, for instance, is a constituent part of Christianity, one of its defining characteristics. 'How often shall I forgive my brother?' Jesus was asked. 'Until seventy times seven,' said Jesus; in other words, endlessly. So a Christian community would combine a high level of moral aspiration and a high level of tolerance and forgiveness. And one interesting note, there will be a particular aversion to cruelty among Christians.

Brice Why is that?

Richard Because it is the worst of the vices, the desire to hurt others, delight, take pleasure, in doing so. It's the exact opposite of loving our neighbour.

Brice That seems very general. Can't you be more specific?

Richard No, that's up to you. You have to take the principles, the great ethical aspirations, and apply them to particular situations and particular people. If you try it you won't find it particularly easy, but no one said Christianity was a piece of cake. You'll need God's help.

Brice As an example, let's talk about sex . . .

Richard Christians seem to have a problem with sex. Why is this? It's something we should try to get clear. What's your angle?

Brice We are spiritual as well as physical beings (this model is a limiting one, but, thanks to the French philosopher and mathematician René Descartes, we are rather stuck with it) and it puts us under a powerful creative tension. If we can't bear the tension we might be inclined to split the two elements up and discard one.

Richard Is this a version of the passion/mind thing you mentioned earlier?

Brice Very much so, and the interesting thing is that, as we've seen before, our spirituality dwells in the space between the two.

If we discard either, we lose the space and so deny a piece of our spiritual potential. In the case of sexuality, the split can be seen in the two extremes of human response to the procreation imperative: maximum activity or complete abstinence. The secular embodiment of the non-spiritual attempt to bring the passion and the ability together would be a sort of James Bond figure. 007 was Ian Fleming's fantasy of the perfect life. James Bond was a highly educated and cultured guy who bedded women all over the world. It's not all that evil but it is second best, it's a lonely adolescent fantasy, but at first sight it seems great.

Richard   This leads us to an important point. We need an ethic of development, one that helps people to grow. It is not a question of putting 'right' and 'wrong' labels on certain acts and saying that they are always wrong as such. It is more a question of developing a certain character, a certain way of responding to people. We need an ethic of aspiration, an ideal, if you like, that will win the consent of people rather than a blanket of condemnation that wins their rejection. We won't achieve that if we rattle on about fornication and say nothing about the development of relationships.

Brice   But we are saying that the kind of sex we are having might not be the best that is available to us. We might not be suffering terribly, but we *are* holding ourselves back from maturity. We're not paying enough attention to the wellbeing of ourselves or the other person.

Richard   We could develop a sexual ethic that was pretty close to some of the traditional approaches but the motivating energy would be very different. It would no longer be fear; it would be a kind of aspiration; it would be a kind of ideal, but with a gentleness to the self. We would know that we were sometimes going to slip up and fail.

Brice Without it being a blanket permission for whatever we wanted because the motivation is towards spiritually integrated sexuality and not, as is so often the case, a sexuality that attempts to exist hidden away in a kind of solitary confinement. A solitary confinement encouraged by generations of guilt-ridden preachers and a prurient society.

Richard Can we connect this with the idea of tension that you mentioned earlier? What makes you say that the tension is creative?

Brice I think God puts our humanness under spiritual tension to draw us out into multi-dimensional beings. Imagine you've squeezed a strip of oil paint out of a tube and on to a canvas. It lies there not really making much of itself until someone comes along with a spatula and spreads it out . . .

Richard Under tension . . .

Brice Into a beautiful pattern.

Richard Or person. And yet the Church seems to see the flesh, as mentioned in Paul's letter to the Romans, in tension with the spirit, as though the Devil had a particular entry to it. I can't accept this way of understanding it. The real source of rebellion is the spirit, not the flesh.

Brice And that way of internalizing what Paul said is probably one of the things that makes many churches wary of other creative endeavours like music and fine art. But perhaps that's another story.

The Seven Deadly Sins

Brice We've talked about sin previously, but not much in terms of behaviour. Perhaps, after all the ground we've covered, it would be worth ending in a way that reaches back into that particular Church tradition. Doesn't the Church divide sin up into seven categories somewhere?

Richard You're referring to the Magnificent Seven: the Seven Deadly Sins. There was a time when there was a passion for classifying everything: the Seven Deadly Sins; the Seven Gifts of the Holy Spirit; the Four Cardinal Virtues; or the Three Theological Virtues, well known from Paul's letter to the Corinthians, where he sings his great hymn to love and ends by saying that, 'Faith, hope and charity all abide, but the greatest of these is charity or love.' So these categorizations of virtue and vice are quite useful, but again they raise questions for us and we have to interpret them.

Brice Well, what are the so-called Seven Deadly Sins? And why are they deadly?

Richard I find the best way to remember sins is by making them into an acronym, such as SLAGPEC. This doesn't get them in any order of seriousness, but it does help me commit them to memory. So here goes. SLAGPEC: sloth, lust, anger, gluttony, pride, envy, covetousness. Those are the Seven Deadly Sins. They seem to have been found first as a list in the writings of St Gregory the Great, one of the popes. If you like, we can take a quick romp through them, though they are probably very familiar to you already.

Brice Oh thanks!

Richard Pride is reckoned to be the foundational sin, the fundamental one, and at its root there seems to be an inability to accept one's true nature as dependent on God and, indeed, on other people. The really proud man, in this sense, is the kind of man who is unable to admit he is ever wrong or ever needs the help of other people. It is indeed a deeply tragic sin and many of the great dramas and stories in literature are woven round it. We need an appropriate level of self-love, of valuing the self, a kind of appropriate pride, if you like, but the sin of pride is disproportionate. It is an inability to admit that we are part of a web of relationships and responsibilities. According to Milton's great poem, *Paradise Lost*, it is Lucifer's inability to accept second place to God that plunges him into hell. So pride is definitely a characteristic that infects us all and is worth looking out for.

Brice Do you want a bit of psycho here?

Richard Okay.

Brice Pride like this, when we see it in ourselves or in others, is a cover-up for deeper feelings. But it won't do to call someone like this an arrogant so-and-so and dismiss them. They need the opposite response, they need gentleness and acceptance.

Richard Is that it?

Brice That's all.

Richard Good. Short and pithy, I like that. Covetousness, probably better thought of as avarice, is the desire to have more and more things, or status, or honour. It is one of the things mentioned in the Tenth Commandment: 'thou shalt not covet thy neighbour's wife, nor his ox, nor his ass, nor anything that is thy neighbour's.' We know that this kind of covetousness can lead to all sorts of other dodges and devices. It can lead us to cheat, even to steal, because we desperately want to keep up with our neighbours. So covetousness, again, is an insidious and toxic sin if we let it take hold of us. Pith invited.

Brice Covetousness: longing for something we don't have, because we don't know how to live with the things we do have. Next.

Richard Lust. Clearly and obviously lust relates to sexual desire. I think a distinction ought to be made between ordinary lusty thoughts and sexual longings, and the acting out of these with cold calculating intent. Lust separates the sexual act from emotion and affection, and experiences it on a purely physical level, whereas the Christian ideal of sex, as, indeed, its ideal of anything, is to humanize it, to give it a human quality, so that it becomes an aspect of a relationship with another person and not simply the use of another person as a form of release.

Brice Yup, the thing about lust is that it is driven by fear of intimacy. Lust can exist on its own in the context of our sexuality, hence pornography. When it exists on its own in sexual relationships, there is no relationship, just exploitation.

Richard Keeping the ball rolling, envy. Envy is the fourth of the great deadlies and has been described as 'sorrow at another's good'. In many ways it is the meanest sin in the book. Covetousness leads you to desire what your neighbour possesses: envy makes you sad that your neighbour possesses it. It has been described supremely as 'the sin among equals'. I'm not likely to envy someone who has been made a Prime Minister or a Professor of Neurosurgery, because I'm neither a politician nor a doctor, but I am likely to feel envy towards a brother minister who becomes famous or is made Archbishop of Canterbury. Or Pope. It is sorrow at my friend's, my brother's, my sister's good fortune. Envy is the sin we rarely confess. We quite often own up to being very proud or being quite randy, but we rarely, I think, admit to the sin of envy. It does show itself very often by a kind of stricture in the face, for instance, when a friend rushes up to us and says that he has got the promotion we were both longing for. You congratulate him, but you have to draw up your congratulations from a well of bitterness, and it shows in the kind of tight way you smile. Do you have anything to add?

Brice We touched on the destructiveness of envy when we talked about power. Incidentally, people get confused by the difference between envy and jealousy. Jealousy involves three people as distinct from the two necessary in envy. Jealousy comes when our relationship with someone seems threatened by a third person. The third 'person' could be imaginary, or a computer or a boat or a dog, but it's never an attribute, that's envy.

Richard Gluttony is simply the indulgence of our ordinary appetites to a disproportionate degree. The great rule in Christian living, indeed in any appropriate human living, is moderation, what we call temperance, the balanced life. The glutton gets things out of proportion, for whatever reason, and they take over. Of course, we're on your ground here, because it may be that gluttony is an old-fashioned name for addiction, those compulsive habits that characterize so many people today in our consumerist society. The glutton is the person who takes a good thing too far, eats too much, drinks too much, smokes too much, talks too much. We can be gluttonous in speech, we can be compulsive talkers.

Brice   Gluttons are never satisfied. Whatever they take in is never quite enough. The hollow inside can never be filled. It needs something else.

Richard   Anger. Well, that's something that you have looked at very carefully in this book and I don't want to add very much to what you've said. There is obviously a sense in which anger is an appropriate and healthy emotion, it's the way we are alerted to danger. It is the disturbance we feel when we are being abused or trespassed upon, and so there is an appropriate way of expressing anger. But I suppose the Church must mean by anger what you have described as rage. You did remind us that Scripture tells us it is possible to be angry and not sin, but the kind of anger that is sinful is when the bitterness wells up in us and turns into an explosion of emotion that is indiscriminate in its effect. To live around a really angry person is to be scorched by the heat of their tongue, cut by them. The word sarcasm comes to mind, it comes from a Greek word that means to tear the flesh. The sarcastic person sends out little hooks of venom, tears at one with remarks that can be extremely painful, especially for the shy or the young, if they sit under a sarcastic or angry teacher. So anger is a grim sin and, of course, it can lead to passion and the kind of abuse of others that ultimately can even take their lives from them; so it, too, is a deadly sin. Sloth is really the sin of inactivity. It's closely related in spiritual writing to despair, and maybe as a shrink you will see connections between it and depression, certain kinds of illness that immobilize us and we sink into a kind of despairing inactivity. Inasmuch as we can do nothing about it, it's a sickness and it ceases to be a sin. But we are drawn, many of us, to inactivity when we should be active and this, of course, is not simply getting up and bustling about in the morning. Many people are very active in that way, but they are morally slothful, they do not take a stand against unrighteousness, they do not defend the weak and the victims. One of my favourite epigrams is from the statesman and political theorist Edmund Burke, who said, 'The only thing needed for the triumph of evil is for good men to do nothing'. And very often good men have a kind of natural easy-going laziness about them, but it can become sinful.

Brice I think there should be an eighth deadly sin: overactivity. Manic activity defends us against our real needs for peace and restoration. I get overactive when I'm afraid no one cares about me. Ironically, it pushes them away, and it pushes God away. Some churches are good at this one.

Richard So these are the Seven, or eight, Deadly sins: deadly because they can lead to real spiritual death in us.

Brice What about these virtues you were talking about?

Richard There's a bit of an overlap between them. In some ways I've already touched upon the Four Cardinal Virtues in expounding the Seven Deadly Sins. The Four Cardinal Virtues are prudence, temperance, fortitude and justice. Prudence is a great capacity, a useful virtue for bishops and diplomats, though I conspicuously lack it. It's a kind of wisdom of utterance, a wisdom in behaviour. The opposite, I suppose, is rashness and impulsiveness. The prudent person calculates, not in a weak and cowardly way, but in a wise way, knowing that very often good intentions can have unintended consequences; so the prudent person is the person who acts wisely. Temperance we have already looked at. It's that gift for moderation, getting the happy medium between excess and a complete absence of a thing. Fortitude, in many ways, is the basis of all virtue. It's the virtue of courage. It takes courage, very often, to stand against the crowd, courage to oppose evil, courage to disagree with the prevailing opinion. Fortitude has that sense of courage and there is a sense of continuity and endurance attached to it. And, of course, justice, which is, along with love or charity, the great Christian desire that all be treated equally so that the kind of divisions that characterize and disfigure human history will be done away, so that all will be treated as ends in themselves, as God's children. So the great virtue of justice treats people even-handedly. Very often we don't do this. St James, in his letter in the New Testament, points out that this wasn't practised very convincingly in the early Church. He points to the fact that if a very rich man comes to church they are immediately all over him, but if a very poor person comes he doesn't get the same reception. The just person treats everyone equally, with what the old prayer book called impartiality. These are quite useful divisions. You mustn't apply any of them absolutely legalistically, but they do help us because human beings like to subdivide and categorize. They help us to identify, in our periods of self-examination, where we are going wrong, where we need to make a little more effort, where we need understanding, and always, where we need forgiveness.

Life After Death

Brice We've spent all of this book, or most if it, in talking about following Christ in this life. Do you want to say anything in conclusion about life after death?

Richard It would certainly be an appropriate way to end, though I'm a little suspicious of using the word 'end' as a way into the topic.

Brice Why is that?

Richard Because it suggests discontinuity, and Christians believe that their life in Christ is a reality so large and important that not even death interrupts it. As we are at present, death is obviously something that we cannot see beyond. We trust that God, who is not trapped in time as we are, will continue to be with us beyond that great horizon. This brings me to the most important, the only really important point, that Christians make about life after death. Christian philosophers use a phrase to describe the created order, including human beings. They say it is contingent. That's really only a sophisticated way of saying that we are all dependent upon the creative and sustaining energy of God for our life. We have not talked much about creation in this book, but modern science shows how exciting and miraculous it is. We now know that all the matter in the universe, which is continually expanding, came from a microscopic dot of potentiality that could slip through the eye of a needle. It exploded, in what scientists call the Big Bang, into our expanding universe. We come, quite literally, from nothing, except the thought of God. There's a lovely African American play called *Green Pastures*, which pictures God as a magnificent black preacher looking out from heaven and saying 'Let's make a world'. Christians believe that the created universe is the result of the overflowing of God's passion; his desire to love and to share his eternal being with creatures made in his image.

Brice And the point you are coming to?

Richard The point I'm coming to is that we are contingent beings, dependent creatures, here at all because God said 'Let there be'. While we cannot understand how the universe came from nothing, the evidence of our own senses and the fact of our own existence proves that it happened. We cannot understand how we can go from the nothingness of death, the dissolution of our bodies into dust, into that eternal life that Christ certainly promised us; but it would be no greater miracle than our original creation.

Brice   You are saying, in fact, that our hope is not in ourselves but in God.

Richard   Absolutely. This is why Christians don't much like to talk of life after death. It suggests some kind of human continuity, as though our own destiny after death were an intrinsic part of our nature. We believe, rather, that our dependence on God continues after death; that the God who brought us out of nothingness into life will not leave us in the nothingness of death. We believe that he will bring us into newer, possibly more developed, ways of being that are clearly not dependent on, or expressed through, our material bodies. One of the wonderful things about modern scientific studies is that they make it easier for us to approach an understanding of this. Nineteenth-century science, in particular, was very materialistic and mechanistic. It tended to emphasize that reality was thick and solid, a thing you could stub your toe on, or stick a knife into. We now realize that the building blocks of the universe are hardly material at all. Someone once described atoms as little bits of nothing moving very fast. The whole material, mechanistic hypothesis has been exploded by modern physics; mysticism has been reintroduced. There may well be dimensions of reality that we cannot get in touch with. All those traditions of angels and non-material spiritual realities may turn out to be true, in spite of the great assault made upon them by the materialistic sciences.

Brice   Well, thank you for that scientific, mystical rhapsody, but can you come back to the main point you were making?

Richard These modern discoveries do excite me greatly and make me more in awe of the creative energy and wisdom of God. But to come back to my central point. Christians do not believe in life after death. They believe in the God who raises from the dead. This is, for us, the meaning of the resurrection of Christ. That extraordinary event that created the Christian Church.

Brice What do you mean when you say the resurrection *created* the Christian Church?

Richard We all know that the disciples forsook Jesus on Good Friday. Well, the male disciples did. The women, as usual, were made of sterner stuff and they accompanied him to Calvary, but when he was arrested in Gethsemane the disciples all fled; a defeated, dispirited bunch, their leader lost. Later, something happened that changed this bunch of dispirited deserters into witnesses who proclaimed that Jesus was alive, and paid the price for their testimony in beatings and imprisonment and death. Something had happened, some spiritual Big Bang, that transformed them into witnesses to the risen Jesus. The New Testament calls it the resurrection of Jesus Christ from the dead. It is a complex mystery, but in its essence it means that Jesus is not simply a dead hero but a living person in the life of the Church. He lives in his disciples, is their contemporary. This is what turned the earliest followers of Jesus into the Church; a coherent body focused on the living reality of Jesus. They preached Jesus and his resurrection, and this was one reason why the Greek philosophers, to whom Paul preached on Mars Hill, as recorded in the Acts of the Apostles, thought he was preaching two new gods, Jesus and Resurrection. Paul is very interesting in the number of ways he tries to express and explain the resurrection. He uses a number of metaphors for it. He says that the Resurrection of Jesus was a down payment, a first instalment, on the resurrection of the whole created universe. One theologian described it as a telegram from God, a signal to us from God, of his intention for the whole universe, but particularly for us. God's creative, transforming energy will restore us from death to an unimaginably glorious life. But the only main point, the bottom line, as businessmen say, is that it is in God we trust. It is the God who created us and redeemed us who will raise us from the death of nothingness into this abundant life. More than that we cannot and need not say.

Brice So you don't want to describe heaven for me?

Richard No, I don't, because I can't. Heaven will be a closer walk with God, as the old hymn puts it. We'll go deeper into God and maybe the inhibitions and difficulties we experience at the moment will disappear there. Even so, I still think there is some evidence that there will be some sort of progression after death.

Brice That's what you meant when you talked about purgatory, isn't it?

Richard Yes. There is some sense in which we must expect to grow; to be purged, if you like, accustomed to the blazing holiness of God's beauty.

Brice That's interesting stuff. People constantly look for natural evidence of life after death. Is there any that we can trust in?

Richard Well, I would be reluctant to trust in it, even if there were any evidence. As I keep saying, Christians trust in God. Nevertheless, there are some interesting experiences around in human history, to which I give some credence. The whole area of psychic research, for instance: while it is a haven for frauds and charlatans, it still has an irreducible core of authenticity about it and points to the fact that we are complex realities who are not as limited by body and time as some people make out. But, anyway, as I've said so often in this conversation, our trust is in the God who created us in the first place. Hope is the future tense of faith. We hope in the life to come. The faith that we have in God and in Christ in this life is not a hope that is abandoned for life beyond life; it is the future tense of that trust. It is a hope that takes us beyond death into the nearer presence of God.

Epilogue

Richard What would you say to someone who's read what we've said and wanted to know more about the kind of things you've talked about?

Brice The psycho stuff you mean?

Richard Yes. I was hoping that you might recommend some further reading.

Brice I can do that, but only a few gems, people can take responsibility for their own exploration after that. The books I have in mind are some that I have found stimulating and that encouraged me to find out more. A good way into Freud is via *The Psychopathology of Everyday Life* (Penguin 1990). This is a collection of his interpretations of the commonplace and is compelling reading. A definitive collection of Freud's writings is *The Essentials of Psycho-Analysis* (Penguin 1991). Serious readers will find it useful to have two other books beside them if they journey any distance into the theories of the unconscious. These are *The Discovery of the Unconscious* by H. Ellenberger (Penguin 1970) and *A Critical Dictionary of Psychoanalysis* by Charles Rycroft (Penguin 1988). Getting off the classical psychoanalytic beat a bit, but just as stimulating, are the books by Alice Miller, *The Untouched Key* (Virago 1990), *Psychoanalytic Studies of the Personality* by W. Ronald D. Fairbairn (Routledge 1990) and *The Uses of Enchantment* by Bruno Bettelheim (Penguin 1991). The first of these is an exploration of childhood trauma and its relation to adult creativity and destructiveness. The second is a wonderful introduction to the meaning and importance of fairy tales.

Richard Fairy tales?

Brice Yes, very important if you want to think about the way we sort the world out in our heads, how we manage the chaos.

Richard I notice there are no Christian books on your list.

Brice I thought I'd let you have first stab at that one.

Richard Well, I think I can come up with some ideas!

Brice I wonder if you'll begin by mentioning some of your own books.

Richard Funny you should say that. As a matter of fact, I would want to recommend a broad spectrum of religious books. I hope that we have persuaded people that we are not pushing a particular line. Christianity is a great and diverse phenomenon and people will come at it from different angles. Many people are interested in the great Roman Catholic

Church and there are many good books on what Catholics believe. A good general guide would be Rod Strange's book, *What Catholics Believe* (Penguin). Of course, many Catholic writers don't push a particular line at all. For instance, Gerard Hughes' *God of Surprises* (Darton, Longman and Todd 1985) is a book on prayer and the Christian life that is widely read. And Hans Kung's books are for everyone. Try *Credo* (SCM 1993).

Brice   What about your own stuff, eh? Any of it any good?

Richard   The readers will decide . . .

Brice   Oh good grief. Just get on and plug them, I know you're dying to.

Richard   I think I would suggest that three of my books might help. They are *Crossfire* and *Another Country, Another King,* both published by Collins (1988 and 1991 respectively), *Anger, Sex, Doubt and Death* (SPCK 1993) and *The Stranger in the Wings* (SPCK 1994).

Brice   That last one covers some of the stuff we've been looking at here doesn't it?

Richard   Yes.

Brice   Any evangelical books to recommend?

Richard   Lots. John Stott is always worth reading, try *The Contemporary Christian* (IVP 1992). *I Believe in the Church* (Hodder Christian Paperbacks 1989) by another evangelical, David Watson, is clear and authoritative. Alister Mcgrath is worth more than a look; with R.T. France he edited a book called *Evangelical Anglicans* (SPCK 1993) that's useful and his *The*

Genesis of Doctrine (Basil Blackwell 1990) is tough but helpful. Then there is Tom Wright who is very helpful in commending an intelligent and scholarly orthodoxy. Try *Who Is Jesus?*

Brice Anything else?

Richard Yes, Marcus Borg's *Jesus, a New Vision* (SPCK 1993) seems to me to offer a creative alternative to the stand-off between liberals and evangelicals. *I Have My Doubts* by H.M. Kuitert (SCM) is quite demanding, but useful. It was a best-seller in Holland. *Who Told You That You Were Naked?* by John Jacob Raub (St Paul Publications 1992) is good for guilt-ridden Christians. Elizabeth Templeton's *The Strangeness of God* (Arthur James) will make the reader think.

Brice In this book we have tried to be as affirming as possible, to recognize that there are different approaches. We've avoided saying that any particular line has been faxed straight from heaven.

Richard That's right. And the reason for that approach was not a sort of cowardly permissiveness or fear of taking sides. It comes, rather, from our recognition that people do vary in their approach to faith in the one God, as mountaineers will tackle an ascent via different faces of the mountain. Taken together, they can give us a fuller picture of God and God's way with us. I hope this book has helped do the same thing.

Brice So do I.